PRAISE FOR MOVING IN THE APOSTOLIC

Exciting news of the restoration of apostles to the Church makes fulfillment of the Great Commission seem suddenly within our reach! John Eckhardt's profound insights into the apostolic ministry will help us all prepare for the coming harvest—and the return of the King.

Dutch Sheets
AUTHOR OF *THE RIVER OF GOD*
PASTOR, SPRINGS HARVEST FELLOWSHIP
COLORADO SPRINGS, COLORADO

There has been a proclamation from heaven of new things into the earth. Vast changes taking place throughout the global Church are moving us into new dimensions of understanding, perception, faith and partnership with God to bring forcefully the purposes of God into full maturity in the earth.
A new vocabulary is arising in the Church as the apostolic servants of the Lord capture the ancient frequencies of the building power of God within the modern contexts of our time. John Eckhardt has traveled the earth trumpeting the new proximity of the presence of the Lord and hammering out the shapes of new understanding and clear teaching in many spiritual battlefields across the earth.
I encourage pastors and leaders not only to read this book, but to teach these principles in their churches and ministries in order to release the apostolic dimension within the hearts of all saints. There is an impartational power in the apostolic anointing which will come upon you as you open your hearts and minds to receive these truths.

Noel Woodroffe
FOUNDER AND APOSTOLIC TEAM LEADER
WORLD BREAKTHROUGH NETWORK
SENIOR ELDER, ELIJAH CENTRE
TRINIDAD, WEST INDIES

Praise for Moving in the Apostolic

Prophetic revelation of Scripture pours through John Eckhardt as he writes about the apostolic dimension—what it is, what it does and what it means to be a "sent one." Apostle John Eckhardt is destined to be known as an apostolic statesman of the twenty-first century.

Mary Crum

FOUNDER AND COPASTOR, LIFE CENTER FAMILY CHURCH
ATLANTA, GEORGIA

John Eckhardt presents genuine revelation of the role and anointing of apostolic ministry in the modern Church. I highly recommend *Moving in the Apostolic.*

Ted Haggard

SENIOR PASTOR, NEW LIFE CHURCH
COLORADO SPRINGS, COLORADO

Cutting-edge truth and a prophetic view of the Church's historical and apostolic birthright are brought forth with revelation and discernment to prepare us for the next millennium. I highly recommend *Moving in the Apostolic* to the whole Body of Christ.

Ivory L. Hopkins

APOSTLE, PILGRIM'S MINISTRY OF DELIVERANCE
HARBESON, DELAWARE

John Eckhardt's *Moving in the Apostolic* is revelatory teaching. This book will help set in order the ministry of the apostle in the Church today. Every pastor and ministry leader should read this book.

Cindy Jacobs

COFOUNDER, GENERALS OF INTERCESSION
COLORADO SPRINGS, COLORADO

Praise for Moving in the Apostolic

John Eckhardt has provided us an excellent comprehensive study on true apostolic ministry—what it is and what it is not. This book is a solid foundation, which will be helpful to all people who desire to embrace the restoration of apostolic ministry to the local church. I, too, agree with John when he states that the restoration of the apostolic to the Church is a key factor in accomplishing the Great Commission—a mission we all want to see fulfilled!

John P. Kelly
FOUNDER AND OVERSEEING APOSTLE
ANTIOCH CHURCHES AND MINISTRIES
SOUTHLAKE, TEXAS

Apostle John Eckhardt draws on his experience as a pioneer of the New Apostolic Reformation to show the necessity for the Church to receive God's restoration of the ministry gift of the apostle. The truths revealed herein will cause the Body of Christ to understand why there cannot be completion—or even a "restitution of all things"—until this gift has been fully restored to the Church. The Spirit of God is now raising up New Testament apostles such as John Eckhardt to prepare us for the new millennium. This book is a must for all believers.

Ernest Leonard
FOUNDER AND PRESIDENT, SCHOOL OF THE APOSTLES
PROVISION OF PROMISE MINISTRIES

Apostle John Eckhardt succinctly and accurately captures the key ingredient to twenty-first century Kingdom dominion—namely the restoration of the authority and power of apostolic commission upon the life of every believer.

Bishop Harold Calvin Ray
PASTOR, REDEMPTIVE LIFE FELLOWSHIP
WEST PALM BEACH, FLORIDA

Moving in the Apostolic

MOVING IN
APOSTOLIC
THE

JOHN ECKHARDT

Renew

A Division of Gospel Light
Ventura, California, U.S.A.

Published by Renew Books
A Division of Gospel Light
Ventura, California, U.S.A.
Printed in U.S.A.

Renew Books is a ministry of Gospel Light, an evangelical Christian publisher dedicated to serv-
ing the local church. We believe God's vision for Gospel Light is to provide church leaders with
biblical, user-friendly materials that will help them evangelize, disciple and minister to children,
youth and families.

It is our prayer that this Renew book will help you discover biblical truth for your own life and
help you meet the needs of others. May God richly bless you.

For a free catalog of resources from Renew Books and Gospel Light please call your Christian supplier,
or contact us at 1-800-4-GOSPEL or at www.gospellight.com.

Cover Design by Kevin Keller • Interior Design by Robert Williams
Edited by Kathi Mills and David Webb

Library of Congress Cataloging-in-Publication Data
Eckhardt, John, 1957–
Moving in the apostolic / John Eckhardt.
    p.   cm.
ISBN 0-8307-2373-0 (trade paper)
1. Apostolate (Christian theology). I. Title.
BV601.2.E35 1999   98-45962
262'.1—dc21   CIP

1 2 3 4 5 6 7 8 9 10 11 12 13 14 15 16 17 18 19 20 / 04 03 02 01 00 99 98

Rights for publishing this book in other languages are contracted by Gospel Literature International
(GLINT). GLINT also provides technical help for the adaptation, translation and publishing of Bible
study resources and books in scores of languages worldwide. For further information, write to GLINT
at P.O. Box 4060, Ontario, CA 91761-1003, U.S.A. You may also send e-mail to Glintint@aol.com, or
visit their web site at www.glint.org.

> "In this point could never our enemies cause us to faint, for our First Petition was, that the reverend face of the Primitive and Apostolic Church should be brought back again to the eyes and knowledge of men."
>
> John Knox
> On the Reformation in Scotland

CONTENTS

FOREWORD

God has begun reinstating the gift and the office of apostle in the 1990s.

This may sound at first like a simple statement, but its implications are profound. The Body of Christ is in a substantially more complete form than it has been, perhaps since New Testament times. This means that God is now prepared to do things through His people here on earth that He has been postponing for a very long time.

As a starter, this decade has been characterized by more quantity, intensity and sophistication of activities involving aggressive spiritual warfare than ever before in recorded history, including the book of Acts. Parallel to this are new levels of prayer, specifically intercession and prophecy. Partially as a result of this, we now live in the first generation of Christians ever to see light at the end of the tunnel of the Great Commission. No previous generation could even *measure* the remaining task, let alone realistically plan to *finish* it!

The restoration of the ministry of apostles to the Body of Christ is directly related to this good news. By this I do not mean that there have not been apostles through the centuries of Christian history. There certainly have been, even though many of them would not have used the title "apostle" to describe themselves. But what I do mean is that the Church as a whole did not recognize the crucial role of apostles; they did not understand it.

Therefore, they were unable to bless it, accept it and relate to it in a godly way. For one thing—check the libraries—books like this one were not on the required reading lists of Christian leaders.

I certainly will require it of my Fuller Seminary students. I want them to get to know my good friend John Eckhardt. I want many of them to say, "John Eckhardt is my role model for ministry today." I am gratified that a rapidly growing number of leaders are now beginning to move in the apostolic gift and the apostolic office. But not all of them will have the ability to stand back, see what they are doing in the broad picture, analyze what is happening through them and exercise the self-discipline to organize their thoughts and put them into book form as John Eckhardt has done. This is not to put the others down. They are highly effective practitioners, and they are advancing the kingdom of God in an awesome manner. John Eckhardt just happens to have both the gift of apostle and the gift of teacher.

From the first page on, John Eckhardt focuses his whole book on the completion of Jesus' Great Commission. Nothing could please me more! Too many Christian leaders become so infatuated by the manifestations of the Holy Spirit, the remarkable advances in Christian unity, the drama of spiritual warfare, the evident signs of revival and the excitement of power evangelism that these are in danger of becoming ends in themselves. For God, they are not ends in themselves, but means toward the end of getting lost souls saved. As you read this book, Apostle Eckhardt will not let you forget this incredibly important truth.

The current literature we have on the ministry of apostles is excellent. But *Moving in the Apostolic* is not a repetition or a rehash of what the other authors are saying. This is the first of our current books written by one who takes his personal role so seriously that he uses the title "Apostle John Eckhardt" without apology. As a result, this book, more than any of the others, lets you go backstage, so to speak, and see just what is going on in the heart and the mind of a true apostle. I have no doubt that as a direct consequence of this book a number of other apostles who may have been a bit timid will find themselves gaining the courage to use the title "apostle" as well. I don't see this as a trivial thing, because I believe that the biblical *office* of apostle carries a dimension of power with it that the *function* alone cannot attain.

My favorite segment of the book is the chapter on warfare. All the apostles I know would agree with John that a primary role of apostle is to lead the Body of Christ out into aggressive spiritual warfare. But none of them have said it as well! If you are a browser who hardly ever reads a whole book, I recommend that you start with that chapter. It is powerful!

I do hope, however, that you and others will read the entire book—not just once, but several times. When these truths penetrate your heart and mind and the hearts and minds of Christian leaders across the board, the day for actually fulfilling the Great Commission will be right around the corner! I want to be here when it happens, and I know that you do, too.

C. Peter Wagner
Cofounder, World Prayer Center

A TIME TO REVIEW

If you are thinking, *This book can't be for me. After all, I'm not an apostle, so I can't get anything out of reading a book about apostles,* think again! Have you ever read the book of Acts and marveled at the power that seemed to be resident in the Early Church, yet come away puzzled at the obvious lack of power in the Church today? Or how about Jesus' words in John 14:12?

> Most assuredly, I say to you, he who believes in Me, the works that I do he will do also; and greater works than these he will do, because I go to My Father.

Have you ever wondered why we just don't see the fulfillment of that promise in the Church today? Have you prayed and fasted and beat your hands bloody against the gates of heaven, only to have your prayers bounce back and lie dormant, seemingly unheard and unanswered, at your feet? Because if you have, you're not alone.

God is stirring up in His people a discontent with the average, run-of-the-mill, status quo Christianity that has sufficed, for the most part, since the deaths of the early apostles. God is calling His Church to step out of mediocrity and into the fullness of its calling and heritage, that the Great Commission might finally be fulfilled and the glorious return of Christ realized. But that will only happen through the restoration of the apostolic ministry and an aggressive appropriation of all that means to the end-times Church.

For that reason, I can say with confidence that if you are a part of the Church, this book is for you. Because, you see, it is time for the Church to review the ministry of the apostolic. To review means to look over, study or examine *again*. Many have studied this ministry from a historical perspective and concluded that the apostolic age of the Church ended with the deaths of the twelve apostles. According to such, we are therefore living in a day when there are no more apostles. In other words, there is no such thing as a current apostolic ministry.

The Holy Spirit, however, is causing many in the Church to take another look at this ministry. By doing so, we are beginning to see things that have been previously hidden from our view. This is why we need a review. By looking again, we will see things we have never seen, and we will see things that were previously seen in a whole new light. Many will want to readjust their thinking and teaching.

Consider what I say, and may the Lord give you understanding in all things (2 Tim. 2:7).

You cannot receive understanding unless you consider what is being said. To consider means to look at thoughtfully. Some will not even consider that apostolic ministry is for today. Their minds are set on believing that the apostolic ministry ceased with the deaths of the twelve. Some will not even consider that there are apostles alive and ministering today. But we cannot be closed-minded and expect the Holy Spirit to teach us new things. Revelation and understanding come to those who consider what is being said. Please take into consideration what is said in this book, and I pray that the Lord will give you understanding in all things.

THE APOSTOLIC COMMISSION: MISSION IMPOSSIBLE?

"Go therefore and make disciples of all the nations,
baptizing them in the name of the Father and of the Son
and of the Holy Spirit, teaching them to observe all
things that I have commanded you; and lo, I am with
you always, even to the end of the age." Amen.
MATTHEW 28:19,20

And He said to them, "Go into all the world and
preach the gospel to every creature."
MARK 16:15

"Mission: Impossible" was a popular espionage series originally broadcast on network television from 1966 to 1973 and recently turned into a blockbuster movie. Each week, the Impossible Missions Force (IMF), a small group of highly trained men and women, was sent on a seemingly impossible mission. Each episode concluded, however, with the mission accomplished despite overwhelming odds. What kept viewers riveted to the program was the ability of the team to encounter and overcome each challenge that stood in the way of completing the mission.

This chapter opens with what is commonly referred to as the Great Commission. It was given to a small group of men, chosen by the Lord, whom He called *apostles*. The mission given by our Lord to the remaining eleven apostles (the twelfth, Judas Iscariot, had killed himself) reminds me of an episode of "Mission: Impossible." These were the same men who had forsaken Jesus and fled at His crucifixion. They had hidden themselves in a room for fear they would share His fate. How could this small, frightened, ragtag group of Galileans fulfill such a Great Commission? How could they overcome the impossible odds stacked against them? How would people believe that their Sender had died and risen from the dead? What would give them the ability to complete such a mission?

Can you relate? Have you ever felt that what God has called you to do—or maybe what you secretly dream of doing for God and His kingdom—is an impossible mission? Do you despair of ever seeing it accomplished? Is it truly hopeless? Or is there, within the apostolic dimension, an answer for you, as surely as there was for the original apostles?

Those same men, who once cowered in fear, eventually went out and, in the face of overwhelming odds, turned their world upside down. The book of Acts is a chronicle of their exploits in the midst of staggering persecution and opposition. How were they able to do it? What was the key to fulfilling their Mission: Impossible?

They Were Sent

Before you respond with the usual, obvious answers of "prayer" and "the power of the Holy Spirit," I want to give you what I believe is an important, yet often overlooked key. As a matter of fact, I consider it to be vital to fulfilling the Great Commission today. This key is so important that I have spent almost ten years of my life studying and preaching on it. The only reason this time span has not been longer is simply because I did not discover this key earlier. I never heard much preaching on it; the Church did not emphasize it.

What is the key? The answer is very simple: *They were sent.*

Now, that may not sound very profound, but I assure you that upon studying what it means to be sent, you will see its importance and understand why the Church has struggled at times in its attempts to fulfill the Great Commission. The purpose of writing this book is to bring understanding to the whole Body of Christ of what it means to be sent, so that each of us may then go forth and fulfill what God has called and gifted and equipped us to do.

To be an apostle, or to be apostolic, revolves around the concept of being sent. Only sent ones can fulfill the Great Commission. Only sent ones will be able to overcome the impossible odds that stand in the way of being able to say, "Mission accomplished." The Church cannot succeed without operating strongly in this dimension.

There are several premises I want to put forth concerning this commission:

1. The Church has been given a commission.
2. This commission is an apostolic commission.
3. This commission must and will be fulfilled.
4. Since the commission is apostolic, it will take an apostolic anointing to fulfill it.

What does it mean to be apostolic? Can we *all* be apostolic? What part do apostles have in fulfilling the Great Commission? When do we receive and operate in an apostolic anointing? How is the Church affected by apostolic ministry? These are some of the questions we will attempt to answer together.

Let's first define the term *commission*. A commission is simply the matter or task so authorized. This means that the task has been authorized by someone with authority. Jesus authorized the apostles to go into all the world to preach. He authorized them to teach and make disciples of all nations (literally, all people groups).

To commission means to authorize, appoint, charge, empower, dispatch and entrust with a mission. This commission was directly given to the apostles but indirectly given to the Church in every generation. It was not just the apostles' commission, but it is our commission today. After the early apostles died, the commission remained. It has yet to be totally fulfilled and will remain in force until the day it is fulfilled.

They Were Given Power and Authority

This assignment means much more than evangelizing. Evangelism is only the beginning of the task. Converts must be discipled. Churches must be planted. Elders must be ordained. The saints must be perfected. As a matter of fact, the work begins before evangelism takes place. Strategic prayer must come first in order to bind the powers of darkness that would hinder evangelism.

THE CHURCH IN THE BOOK OF ACTS WAS FIRST AND FOREMOST AN APOSTOLIC CHURCH.

Evil spirits must be dealt with. Prophetic utterances must be released. Many have believed the commission is an evangelistic commission. Although evangelism is an important part, the commission is essentially *apostolic*, incorporating evangelism to fulfill it. Sent ones do more than evangelize. Sent ones preach, teach, prophesy and do the works of Jesus.

The commission is apostolic because it was originally given to the apostles. It was given and received in this context. The

Church in the book of Acts was first and foremost an apostolic Church. They understood that they were sent ones. They knew that they were authorized to carry out this mission. The dominant anointing in the book of Acts was apostolic, and it was the anointing that governed what they did. The apostolic set the tone for the Early Church; it molded who they were and what they did.

When I say the commission was apostolic, I mean it was given to sent ones. This is the basic definition of the word *apostle*. It is taken from the Greek word *apostolos*, meaning a delegate, an ambassador of the gospel, officially a commissioner of Christ (with miraculous powers), messenger, *he that is sent*. Before this word found its way into our Bible, it was a secular term used by the Greeks and Romans to describe special envoys who were sent out for the purpose of expanding the dominion of the empire.

Many of these envoys were military generals with authority to go into new territories and fight, if necessary, to establish the Greek or Roman culture in that region. They were also responsible for teaching and training the new subjects in the laws and culture of the kingdom.

These envoys were given power and authority from the king to fulfill their mission. They were responsible for fulfilling their commissions and were given everything they needed to succeed. They were highly intelligent and gifted individuals, specially chosen for the task. They were sent to certain territories and charged to subdue, conquer, convert, instruct, train and establish the new subjects in the culture of the empire.

This word *apostle* has been a part of the Church since the days our Lord ministered on the earth. It now describes the commission given to the first apostles. They were sent into the territories of the earth to convert multitudes of people and incorporate them into the kingdom of God. They were given power and authority to accomplish the task. They were responsible for teaching, training and instructing the new believers, making them productive citizens of the Kingdom.

Apostles were sent to establish the Kingdom in the hearts of people and to establish churches throughout the world. They were given the power of the Holy Spirit to help them fulfill this mission.

If the commission is apostolic, that means only sent ones can fulfill it. Every church and every believer must have this dimension to be a part of fulfilling the Great Commission. This does not make everyone an apostle, but everyone can be *apostolic*. The Church therefore needs to be first and foremost an apostolic Church if it is to fulfill its mission.

The Apostolic Spirit

"But the Helper, the Holy Spirit, whom the Father will send in My name, He will teach you all things, and bring to your remembrance all things that I said to you" (John 14:26).

The Holy Spirit is an apostolic Spirit. He is apostolic because He has been *sent* by the Father. He is also a prophetic Spirit, for when He comes the sons, daughters, servants and handmaidens will prophesy (see Acts 2:17,18). He is an evangelistic Spirit because He convicts and draws sinners to Christ (see John 16:8,9). He is a pastoral Spirit because He appoints overseers for the saints (see Acts 20:28). He is a teaching Spirit according to 1 John 2:27.

All believers who have received the Holy Spirit have within them these dimensions. Those believers called to the fivefold ministry (see Eph. 4:11,12) will have a greater dimension of the Holy Spirit's anointing in the gift to which they are called. The apostles will have a greater measure of the apostolic dimension upon their lives to impart and stir up this anointing in the saints.

It is the responsibility of the apostles to release and stir up the apostolic dimension in every believer through teaching, preaching, prophesying and the laying on of hands. When saints become aware of and begin to walk in this dimension of the Spirit, they will manifest the power, authority and characteristics of a sent one.

Jesus the Apostle was sent by the Father, and His words indicated His awareness of that apostleship (see John 3:34; 5:22-30; 6:38-44).

A characteristic of the apostolic spirit is an *awareness* of being sent. There is a sense of purpose and destiny that results from the apostolic spirit—a focus upon fulfilling a divine commission. All ministers are sent by the Lord (see Rom. 10:15), but the very heartbeat of apostleship is the concept of being sent.

When the Church loses this dimension, it loses its sense of divine purpose and mission. Whole denominations dry up and decline because of the absence of the apostolic anointing. After the death of the early apostles, the Church became institutional and ceremonial. The apostolic spirit is necessary for the Church to fulfill the Great Commission to go into all the world and preach the gospel to every creature (see Mark 16:15).

> So Jesus said to them again, "Peace to you! As the Father has sent Me, I also send you." And when He had said this, He breathed on them, and said to them, "Receive the Holy Spirit" (John 20:21,22).

Jesus compared the sending of the apostles to His being sent by the Father. He then breathed on them that they might receive the Holy Spirit—an apostolic Spirit. We know that Jesus, as an Apostle, is in a class by Himself. However, many similarities and characteristics of His being sent apply to the apostolic anointing today. The attributes of a sent one should be found in every believer. This is based upon the words of our Lord as reviewed in this text. As we meditate on these words, we will begin to see the apostolic dimension clearly.

As you read this book, your mission, should you choose to accept it, is to receive clarity and understanding concerning apostles and apostolic people; learn to flow and operate in this dimension; and become an active part of fulfilling the mission given to the Church.

Unlike the Impossible Missions Force, you can rest assured that, no matter what happens, the Lord your God will never leave you nor disavow you (see Deut. 31:6). This page will self-destruct in five seconds. God go with you, sent one.

CHAPTER TWO

THE RESTORATION
OF APOSTOLIC
MINISTRY

Repent therefore and be converted, that
your sins may be blotted out, so that times of refreshing
may come from the presence of the Lord, and that
He may send Jesus Christ, who was preached to you
before, whom heaven must receive until the times
of restoration of all things, which God has spoken by the
mouth of all His holy prophets since
the world began.

ACTS 3:19-21

These verses speak of times of refreshing and times of restoration. There are seasons when God refreshes His people, and also seasons when God restores truths and ministries that have been lost through sin, neglect and tradition. We are now in a time of restoration (or "restitution," as the *King James Version* reads) of apostolic ministry to the Church. The word *restitution* comes from the Greek word *apokatastasis*, meaning to reconstitute in health, home or organization—to restore again.

As you read this book, keep in mind that God wants to bring restoration and restitution to your life, in personal areas as well as in areas of ministry. Pray and ask God to help you identify these areas as you read, and then make yourself available for God to work that restoration in and through you to others.

A Necessary Change

To restore means to bring back into existence or use; to reestablish, to bring back to an original condition. It means to put back, replace, reinstate, reinstall, revive, recall to life, return, to rebuild in a form supposed to be the original. This implies that there has been a departure from the original design. Things fall apart and deteriorate through neglect; decline is inevitable without constant upgrade and renovation. Restoration is then necessary to correct and change the situation.

This is why some people so enjoy buying an older home and then going through the arduous process of restoring the home to its original condition. Although run-down and deteriorated, it is obvious to the perceptive eye that the house once had an elegance and charm that can be restored once again. These perceptive people relish both the process and the results of that restoration. In a sense, they exercise mercy on the old house and enter into the work of lovingly restoring it.

Restoration within the Church—and that includes each of us personally—will happen as a result of God's mercy. He will not allow us to languish in the deterioration of the past. Because of His great love, He restores to us what we need to fulfill His plans and purposes for the earth.

The prophets spoke of restoration. The Weymouth translation says restoration is that "of which God has spoken from the earliest ages through the lips of His holy prophets" (Acts 3:21).

> Be glad then, you children of Zion, and rejoice in the Lord your God; for He has given you the former rain faithfully,

and He will cause the rain to come down for you—the former rain, and the latter rain in the first month.

So I will *restore* to you the *years* that the swarming locust has eaten, the crawling locust, the consuming locust, and the chewing locust, My great army which I sent among you (Joel 2:23,25, *NKJV*, emphasis added).

Joel declared a part of what would happen in the last days. We are now experiencing the greatest outpouring of the Holy Spirit the world has ever known. There are more Spirit-filled believers alive today than at any other time in history. In the midst of this outpouring comes restoration. Apostolic ministry is being discussed around the world. Some are rejecting it altogether, but many are embracing it and beginning to walk in it. It is something fresh. It is the new thing that God is doing.

I have emphasized the words *restore* and *years* in Joel's prophecy. Not only is God restoring apostolic ministry to the Church, but He is also restoring the years that were lost during the relative absence of this important office. In other words, the harvest of souls that was lost during these years will be reaped in our lifetime. We will see multitudes swept into the kingdom as a result of this end-times move of the Holy Spirit.

But this is a people robbed and plundered; all of them are snared in holes, and they are hidden in prison houses; they are for prey, and no one delivers; for plunder, and no one says, "Restore!" (Isa. 42:22).

The Church is now crying out for the restoration of authentic apostolic ministry. We are praying for restoration and declaring it prophetically. God's people are coming out of the holes and prison houses. A new liberty is coming to the Church. A new freedom in ministry is being released through the restoration of apostolic ministry.

Restoration is necessary because of the "departure" (i.e., gradual decline) of authentic apostolic ministry after the death of the early apostles. Paul warned the Church of what would happen when he departed. A picture of what happens when apostolic ministry is no longer present, this prophecy came to pass after the death of the early apostles.

> For I know this, that after my departure savage wolves will come in among you, not sparing the flock. Also from among yourselves men will rise up, speaking perverse things, to draw away the disciples after themselves (Acts 20:29,30).

As early as the second and third centuries, the Church drifted into ceremonialism and tradition. False teaching almost drowned out the truth. Eventually the Church entered the period called the Middle Ages, a time in which the institutional Church gained immense social and political power, but often departed significantly from true apostolic practice and teaching. Later, the Protestant Reformation of the sixteenth century began to bring the Church out of the spiritual darkness that had blinded the minds of many for centuries.

The Roman Catholic Church taught that the Church was indeed "apostolic," but that Christ's apostolic authority was institutionalized in the succession (or sequence of appointments) of bishops. This authority was believed to have come from Christ, who had appointed the disciples, who had in turn appointed "bishops" (Greek: *episcopos*) over various cities. From the second to the sixteenth centuries, all the leading centers of the Church had bishops. In the Roman Catholic Church, the Pope, the bishop of the church at Rome, came to be recognized as the highest bishop of all.

The Protestant Reformation challenged this monopolistic doctrine. The reformers considered apostolic authority to be found in the Bible alone (*sola scriptura*) rather than in Church tradition and institutions. Unfortunately, many of the most prominent protestant reformers also believed that the apostolic period had ceased at about the same time as the completion of the New Testament.

A Perpetual Ministry

The apostolic office was never designed to cease; it was intended to be a perpetual office throughout the Church age. The eleven apostles understood by the prophecy of David that this office must be filled when vacant.

Let his days be few, and let another take his office (Ps. 109:8).

For it is written in the Book of Psalms: "Let his dwelling place be desolate, and let no one live in it"; and, "Let another take his office" (Acts 1:20)·

The remaining apostles prayed for the Lord's guidance in choosing another to take the place of Judas Iscariot. They understood by the Word of the Lord that another should fill the office vacated by Judas. This is a biblical principle concerning ministry offices. Each generation is responsible to pray and believe God to fill the offices left by the previous generation.

It is not the will of God for these offices to remain vacant. When they are vacant, the Church will suffer because of the absence of the anointing.

The Constitution of the United States provides for the executive office of the president to be filled from generation to generation. When a president vacates the office, another replaces him by election or appointment. If the president dies while in office, there is an order of succession, beginning with the vice president, to fill the position.

The office of the president did not cease with the death of George Washington. We would not think of leaving the office of the president vacant. Someone must stand in this office to execute the affairs of the government. The same is true concerning the Church. Although the office of the apostle has been vacant at times because of the unbelief and tradition of the Church, it is now being filled again by those chosen of the Lord. Our doctrine is being corrected, and we are crying, "Restore!"

ALTHOUGH THE APOSTOLIC OFFICE HAS BEEN VACANT BECAUSE OF THE UNBELIEF AND TRADITION OF THE CHURCH, IT IS NOW BEING FILLED AGAIN BY THOSE CHOSEN OF THE LORD.

The ministry of apostleship is perpetual. Although the early apostles died, the office did not. Apostles are officers of the Church. They are not the only officers, but they have an important work. An officer is an executive, and executives have the authority to execute commissions. Since the commission of the Church is apostolic, the Church needs apostles to be able to fulfill it.

An Apostolic Reformer

In 1896, John Alexander Dowie, the founder of the Christian Catholic Church, preached a sermon from his headquarters in Chicago entitled "The Ministry of an Apostle—Is It For Today?" Dowie skillfully demonstrated that those who maintained that there were only twelve apostles could not account for the apostles Matthias, Paul, James (the brother of Jesus), Barnabas, Apollos and others who are called apostles in the book of Acts and throughout the New Testament.

You see, most of the Church of Dowie's day did not believe that the ministry of the apostle continued beyond the deaths of the Twelve who were with Jesus and, of course, the apostle Paul.

Dowie maintained that the ministry of the apostle was a perpetual one, set in the Church by God, until the return of Christ. Amazingly, many in the Church today hold a position similar to that of the Church in Dowie's day.

Dowie maintained that God's order is *first* apostles, *second* prophets, *third* teachers. This was indeed a radical message against the religious tradition of his day. And though many did not like his message, it was nonetheless scriptural and true. Dowie preached a message of the restoration of the apostle to the Church that was ahead of its time.

In addition to his preaching, John Alexander Dowie's ministry was apostolic. He was also a reformer in that he preached a strong message against the apostasy of the Church during his time. An important forerunner of the modern Pentecostal movement, Dowie brought to the Church a message of healing and deliverance that had been obscured for hundreds of years.

Dowie was bitterly opposed by much of the clergy, who called him a fraud for practicing divine healing. He was also opposed by the press and the city of Chicago, which arrested him more than 100 times in 1895 in an attempt to stop his ministry of divine healing. However, the more he was fought, the more successful his ministry became. Hundreds were healed, and thousands came to hear his preaching. He was able to fill up the second largest auditorium in Chicago.

He preached against the hypocrisy of the Church and the evils of tobacco and alcohol in the city. The results were phenomenal! Thousands were saved, and many of his enemies were eventually exposed for their sins. Dowie's ministry shook the city of Chicago and caused trouble in civil and religious circles. He eventually left Chicago and set up his headquarters 40 miles north, naming it Zion.

Dowie's sermons were directed against the denominationalism and sectarianism of the Church of his day. As mentioned earlier, apostles are concerned with the form of the Church. When the form is not according to the Word of God, the apostle will discern it, and preach and teach the Word to bring the Church back into God's proper form.

A strong reforming spirit was present in Dowie's preaching, especially in the area of healing. The Church's lack of practice and faith in this area troubled him. He thought it was hypocritical for the Church not to show compassion toward the sick by praying and believing God for their healing.[1]

The Last-Days Church

Calling a bird of prey from the east, the man who *executes* My counsel, from a far country. Indeed I have spoken it; I will also bring it to pass. I have purposed it; I will also do it (Isa. 46:11, emphasis added).

To execute means to carry out instructions. The apostles were given instructions by the Lord before He left. They were told to go into all the world and preach the gospel to every creature. They were instructed to go and teach all nations. They were also given the power and authority to carry out these instructions.

To execute also means to bring to fruition, to complete, to fulfill. Apostolic ministry is a necessary part of fulfilling the Great Commission. The Church needs apostolic power and authority in order to fulfill and carry out the instructions left by our Lord. Therefore, a restoration of apostolic ministry is absolutely necessary in order for the Church to complete its mission on earth.

And God has appointed these in the church: first apostles, second prophets, third teachers, after that miracles, then gifts of healings, helps, administrations, varieties of tongues (1 Cor. 12:28).

The nineteenth and twentieth centuries have seen 150 years of increasing restoration for the Church. The order of this restoration has roughly corresponded to a reversal of 1 Corinthians 12:28, with the last things restored first and the first last (see Matt. 19:30).

The precursors of the modern restoration were the healing movements in the American holiness movement in the 1830s under Charles Finney and Phoebe Palmer, the 1860s under Dr. Charles Cullis, the Keswick movement (with internationally famous leaders such as William Boardman, A. J. Gordon, R. L. Stanton, R. Kelso Carter, Andrew Murray and A. B. Simpson), Carrie Judd, Maria Woodworth-Etter and John Alexander Dowie.[2]

Diversities of tongues were restored with the outpouring of the Holy Spirit at Azusa Street in Los Angeles (1906-1909). Helps and governments followed with the establishing and structuring of many Pentecostal fellowships, which continued the move of the Holy Spirit.

The 1940s and 1950s saw a further restoration of healing and miracles with the coming of many healing evangelists. The restoration of the teacher came in the 1970s, followed by a strong move of the prophetic in the 1980s. Finally, the 1990s have seen the beginning of the restoration of the apostolic office.

I am not implying that no one walked in the apostolic office before the 1990s. There have always been those who operated under this anointing throughout the history of the Church. I am talking about this office being restored in its fullness. The Lord is putting honor upon the part of the Body that has been lacking (see 1 Cor. 12:24). The Lord is honoring the office of the apostle by putting His glory upon it in this hour. As we honor what God honors, we will receive the blessing and fullness of what the Lord has reserved for the last-days Church.

With the restoration of the office of the apostle, there is a restoration of apostolic doctrine, apostolic binding and loosing, apostolic revelation, apostolic governments and apostolic boldness. According to the prophet Haggai, the glory of the latter temple (the Church) shall be greater than the former (see Hag. 2:9).

The Return of the Ax Head

But as one was cutting down a tree, the iron ax head fell into the water; and he cried out and said, "Alas, master! For it was borrowed." So the man of God said, "Where did it fall?" And he showed him the place. So he cut off a stick, and threw it in there; and he made the iron float. Therefore he said, "Pick it up for yourself." So he reached out his hand and took it (2 Kings 6:5-7).

As the sons of the prophets were cutting down trees to build a house, the ax head fell into the water. This represents the building anointing. You cannot cut down trees and acquire the wood for building without the ax head. The lost ax head represents the anointings that were submerged under religion and tradition for so many years. Through a miracle, the ax head was recovered.

With the apostolic and prophetic anointings being returned to the Church, we are seeing a return of the ax head. These are cutting-edge ministries that give the Church the ability to build.

Elisha instructed the young man to take up the ax head. This is what the Lord is requiring the Church to do in this hour. We must take up the apostolic and prophetic ministries that are coming up from the place of submersion. These anointings are once again coming to the surface. We must not be afraid to pick them up. God is doing His part; now we must do ours.

Notes

1. Dowie was considered by many to be somewhat of a radical, because he insisted that supernatural healing was always instantaneous, and because of his vigorous opposition to the use of physicians and medicine. He became increasingly eccentric later in life, claiming to be the prophesied Elijah, the restorer, in 1901. Stanley M. Burgess and Gary B. McGee, *Dictionary of Pentecostal & Charismatic Movements* (Grand Rapids: Zondervan, 1988), pp. 367, 249.
2. Burgess and McGee, *Dictionary*, pp. 356-367.

CHAPTER THREE

END-TIMES COMMISSION, END-TIMES ANOINTING

Many believers have heard the term "the Great Commission." This is a reference to the words of our Lord Jesus to "Go into all the world and preach the gospel to every creature," and to "make disciples of [teach] all the nations" (Mark 16:15; Matt. 28:19). But though many believers are familiar with the term, not all understand its importance—or their part in its completion.

Preaching the gospel and making disciples throughout the world is not just a job for missionaries; it is an assignment given to all believers. Each of us who has received Jesus Christ as Savior has a part to play in the fulfillment of this commission. However, we cannot successfully fulfill our part without an understanding and appropriation of the apostolic dimension in our lives.

To better understand the necessity of the apostolic dimension in the fulfillment of the Great Commission, let's first define the word *commission*. It means an authoritative order, a charge, a direction. To commission means to *authorize* or to *send on a mission*. Another word synonymous with commission is the word *mandate*. A mandate is an authoritative order or a command.

This commission from our Lord is called the Great Commission for several reasons. These reasons can be found in defining the word *great*, which means unusually or comparatively large in size or dimensions; large in numbers; numerous; unusual or considerable in degree, power, intensity; important; highly significant or consequential. By this definition, there are four reasons why ours is called "the Great Commission":

- Its scope: the largest—the world.
- Its numbers to be touched: multitudes of people.
- Its degree or power: intense.
- Its significance: of primary importance.

The Great Commission is an end-times commission. Never before in history have the means to accomplish this mandate been available to the Church as they are today. We have the technology, the transportation, the publications and the finances needed to accomplish our mission. And now the Lord is also raising up apostolic and prophetic ministry to the nations. These are *end-times anointings* to fulfill this *end-times commission*.

An Apostolic Mandate

As the Lord began to move me into apostolic ministry, I realized that my commission was much larger than the vision I had had. The church I pastor has started several other churches, which we call "Crusaders Churches." Having always had a desire to help raise up supernatural churches, I believe the local church is the greatest weapon against the gates of hell. This is what our Lord prophesied in Matthew 16:18, when He said, "And I also say to you that you are Peter, and on this rock I will build My church, and the gates of Hades shall not prevail against it."

However, my vision for the local church was limited because I did not fully understand the apostolic mandate upon my life. I have been commissioned to do more than plant a church here and there. I have a part to play in fulfilling the Great Commission to the nations of the earth. This commission was given to the apostles by the Lord before His departure. He then sent the Holy Spirit to give them power to be witnesses throughout the world—not just within their city or nation but "unto the *uttermost part of the earth*" (Acts 1:8, *KJV*, emphasis added).

This apostolic mandate is also found in Acts 13:47: "For so the Lord has commanded us: 'I have set you as a light to the Gentiles, that you should be for salvation to the ends of the earth.'" The Norlie translation says, "The Lord gave us a commission." The apostles Barnabas and Paul understood their commission. They understood their ministry as light to the nations. Their ministry carried them beyond the local church at Antioch.

Where did they find this commission? Where did it come from?

It is the prophetic word spoken by Isaiah hundreds of years before: "I will also give You as a light to the Gentiles, that You should be My salvation to the ends of the earth" (Isa. 49:6). Isaiah was prophesying about an end-times commission—and the end-times anointing of the apostles.

On the basis of that prophetic word, Paul and Barnabas went forth to the nations, bringing salvation and deliverance. This commission is to the "ends of the earth." This is the same as the "uttermost part of the earth" spoken by our Lord in Acts 1:8 (*KJV*). The Great Commission is an *apostolic end-times commission* to bring *salvation* to the ends of the earth.

Apostles were *commanded* by the Lord and *set* to be a light to the *Gentiles* (nations). To be set means to be appointed. They were appointed to bring salvation to the uttermost parts of the earth. This carries apostolic ministry beyond the boundaries of the local church. Apostolic ministry brings light (revelation) to the nations, which in turn brings salvation (deliverance).

This is an end-times commission to the nations. Apostolic churches will touch nations. They will be appointed and anointed to fulfill this mandate. The Lord is releasing an end-times apostolic anointing to fulfill the Great Commission.

Local churches will have a part to play in this end-times commission. Just as the churches of Paul's day shared in his ministry through prayer and giving, so it will be in this hour. Local churches must get involved and relate to apostolic ministry. Every local church needs to be a partaker in this end-times commission and end-times anointing. Prophets and prophetic ministry are also a part of this end-times move. Apostles and prophets will need to work together (along with those with other ministry gifts) to fulfill the Great Commission.

Apostles and prophets have a unique ability to penetrate. They carry an authority and power in the Spirit to break through. The traditional way of sending missionaries to foreign lands will not do. Thank God for every missionary who has labored in the field; many have done great works. Many, however, have been sent out by mission boards instead of being sent out by the Lord.

The Lord is raising up a new breed of believers with an end-times apostolic and prophetic anointing to shake nations and establish strong local churches. Much of the work in the past was left to the evangelist. The evangelist would go when no one else would. If it had not been for the office and gift of the evangelist, millions would have been lost and consigned to hell. But even after years of evangelism, many nations still sit in darkness. It will take the end-times anointing of the apostles and prophets to penetrate the darkness.

Together they will bring light where there is presently darkness. They will carry salvation to the ends of the earth. Just as the evangelists were stirred to go to the nations (and will continue to go), the Lord is stirring up the apostles and prophets to go. They are recognizing this end-times commission and end-times anointing.

Dear evangelist, pastor and teacher, don't fight the apostles and prophets the Lord is raising up. They are needed in order to fulfill the Great Commission, just as you are. They have received a commission from the Lord, as well as an anointing to fulfill their mandate. They are beginning to recognize who they are and what their purpose is. They will be a blessing to the Body of Christ and to the nations of the earth.

The Uttermost Part of the Earth

But ye shall receive power, after that the Holy Ghost is come upon you: and ye shall be witnesses unto me both in Jerusalem, and in all Judea, and in Samaria, and unto the uttermost part of the earth (Acts 1:8, *KJV*).

The *New American Standard Bible* translates the scope of our commission as "even to the remotest part of the earth." The Goodspeed translation says "to the very ends of the earth."

Being saved and Spirit-filled in a Pentecostal church, I was always familiar with this verse of Scripture. I heard it preached and quoted often in our church. However, the emphasis was usually on the word "power." We were taught that we needed this power to be effective witnesses. Recently, the Lord led me to preach on this verse. I assumed that every believer knew it because I had heard it so much as a young man.

But this time, as I prepared to preach on it, the Lord impressed me to emphasize the phrase "uttermost part of the earth." The Lord told me that the blessing of Pentecost went beyond what most Spirit-filled believers experience today. The Pentecostal blessing is, in fact, an anointing to touch the world. It is larger than our local church. It is larger than our city or nation. We cannot contain it or limit it to these areas alone.

The outpouring at Azusa Street at the beginning of the twentieth century was the beginning of the release of an end-times anointing for the world. The Lord told me to tell His people that we are not walking in the fullness of this anointing until we are touching the uttermost parts of the earth. If we are just touching a few in our city or region, we are only walking in a part of the power available to us.

The power of the Holy Spirit is given to us to touch nations. We need to prepare believers with a vision for the world. The Lord is now raising up international churches with an apostolic anointing to train and release people in the fullness of the Holy Spirit's power.

An International Anointing

This end-times commission will only be accomplished with an international anointing. Jerusalem on the day of Pentecost was an international setting:

> Then they were all amazed and marveled, saying to one another, "Look, are not all these who speak Galileans? And how is it that we hear, each in our own language in which we were born? Parthians and Medes and Elamites, those dwelling in Mesopotamia, Judea and Cappadocia, Pontus and Asia, Phrygia and Pamphylia, Egypt and the parts of Libya adjoining Cyrene, visitors from Rome, both Jews and proselytes, Cretans and Arabs—we hear them speaking in our own tongues the wonderful works of God" (Acts 2:7-11).

Present here were people from all over the known world. Jerusalem was an international city, and the apostles were receiving an international anointing. Pentecost cannot be limited to any one place. This anointing takes the limits off the Church. It gives us the power and ability to impact all people and nations. It is not by accident that the Pentecostal outpouring of the twentieth century began in America.

I believe the American church has a responsibility to touch

the nations of the earth. Just as America's government cannot limit itself to a domestic policy, but must also have a strong foreign policy, so it is with the Church in America. Every church must have a foreign policy. America cannot excuse itself from the affairs of the world. Neither can the American church. "To whom much is given, from him much will be required" (Luke 12:48).

APOSTOLIC MINISTRY OPERATES AT A RANK HIGH ENOUGH TO SPEAK ON BEHALF OF HEAVEN.

The Lord is raising up spiritual diplomats to execute an end-times foreign policy. He is releasing divine strategies to the Church for the end times. These diplomats are receiving their commission from heaven and are going forth with full authority and power as ambassadors of Christ. This is one of the definitions of the apostle: an "ambassador of Christ." An ambassador is a diplomatic official of the highest rank, sent by a sovereign or state to another as its resident representative.

Notice the definition for ambassador includes the "highest rank"; because of this rank, ambassadors have the authority to speak on behalf of the government that sent them. This is why apostolic anointing is so important for this hour. Apostolic ministry operates at a rank that is high enough to speak on behalf of heaven. Even the principalities and powers must acknowledge this rank because it is spiritual. They hate it and fight against it, but they cannot avoid it or overcome it.

What we need to fulfill the Great Commission are ambassadors and diplomats raised up and sent by the Lord, not people sent by man. The Lord is raising up ambassador churches that will impact the nations of the earth. These will be true international centers that will birth and release ministries into the earth.

First in God's Order

Apostles have been set *first* in the Church by God (see 1 Cor. 12:28). The word "first" is the Greek word *proton,* meaning first in time, place, order or importance; before, at the beginning, chiefly, first of all. This is God's order: first apostles, second prophets, third teachers. I call this the law of first things. When God says first, He means *first.* When we violate this order, we are violating the law of first things.

When you break a law, you will suffer. Many local churches suffer because they have not recognized God's order. A church out of order will not recognize the fullness of God's anointing. The anointing flows through order. The Church Age began with apostles. Many denominations started with apostles. When something begins in the right order, it has a much better chance of success.

It is amazing how many churches do not recognize this order, although it is plainly stated in the Word of God. It's so simple. First means first, second means second, third means third. It's as easy as one, two, three.

The Church was started and birthed through apostolic ministry. Churches today need to be birthed and started through apostolic ministry. Everything has a beginning. This is called the law of Genesis. Everything has a beginning and reproduces after its kind. If something begins wrong, it will usually end wrong. If it begins right, it has a better chance of ending right.

Apostles are usually the first ones to go into a geographical region to preach and to establish and plant churches. They are often the first to preach certain revelations that God is releasing to the Church. Every field of study has apostles or pioneers. For example, there are pioneers in medicine, economics, aviation, law and civil rights. These are the people who make significant breakthroughs in their fields. It is the same in the realm of the spirit.

The apostle Peter was to experience breakthroughs among the Jews, the apostle Paul among the Gentiles. Nations, regions, cities and denominations all have apostles. These are the *first in time* to preach a truth, establish a church or experience a breakthrough in a city, region or nation.

Apostles are also first in rank. This truth may be difficult for some to receive. Many are afraid that some will take this truth to the extreme and end up shipwrecked. However, we need not fear the truth. True apostles must manifest the character of Christ and never use their authority in the wrong way; to do so will bring the judgment of God.

Rank is defined as a degree or position of dignity, eminence or excellence, a grade of official standing. Even though we are all equal in Christ as to salvation, there are different ranks in the spirit. Different ranks carry different degrees of authority and power. Just as there is rank in the military, there is also rank in the army of God. There is rank in the spirit realm. There is rank in the Godhead. There is rank among angels. There is even rank among evil spirits. All authority and power is based upon rank. We must be able to receive, walk in and discern different rankings in the spirit.

Evil spirits recognize spiritual rank. Every believer has rank to cast out devils. Apostles walk and minister in the highest rank. Evil spirits and angels recognize this rank. Apostles have enough rank to command, decree and rebuke with authority. Their rank is within their sphere of authority.

Apostles have rank in the areas they have been assigned by God. They cannot go anywhere and claim rank over anyone. The apostle Paul talked about not going beyond his measure (see 2 Cor. 10:14). The Moffatt translation says, "I am not overstepping the limit, as if you lay beyond my sphere."

We have been guilty of overlooking this order because we have either:

- not been taught it,
- did not see it clearly, or
- simply rejected it.

Tradition has also made this word of no effect (see Mark 7:13). Because of tradition, many would rather call someone a "reverend," a "doctor," a "superintendent" or a "bishop," but seldom an apostle. Those who dared to identify themselves in this way have been considered extreme. Many have ignored, avoided and attacked the office of the apostle. But God is restoring this ministry to the Church and giving us a revelation of its purpose and function. As believers begin to lay hold of this truth, they will also begin to move into the fullness of their calling and be enabled to fulfill their part in the Great Commission.

CHAPTER FOUR

PIONEERING: BACK TO THE BASICS

And God has appointed these in the church:
first apostles, second prophets, third teachers, after
that miracles, then gifts of healings, helps,
administrations, varieties of tongues.

1 CORINTHIANS 12:28

Each and every believer has been gifted by God to fulfill his or her calling and purpose. For some, their gifts will place them in a visible ministry; others are gifted for "behind-the-scenes" ministries. No gift makes anyone more important than anyone else. We are all equal in Christ—equally loved by God and equally necessary to the Body of Christ.

And yet, as we have seen, certain offices within the Church are designated by God as being higher in rank than others. The reason for this is that someone has to be first; someone has to be a pioneer.

What 1 Corinthians 12:28 tells us is that the Church should be first and foremost apostolic. This is the divine order of ministry given to the Church. There is a wisdom behind this order. It is not to elevate men or exalt the flesh. God has a purpose in everything He does.

A Divine Order

Each of the gifts has a certain function that operates best in divine order. When the Church neglects this order, it will not be able to progress toward the goal of fulfilling its commission. When things are out of order, the result is disorder and confusion. The anointing and power of God flow through order. The anointing flowed from Aaron's head, to his beard, to the skirts of his garments (see Ps. 133:2).

The head represents authority. Order is always based on authority. Again, the authority of the Church should be first apostolic, second prophetic, third teaching. The amount of authority we operate in is based on this order. The flow of the anointing is based on this order. Our ability to fulfill the Great Commission is based on this order.

The apostolic prepares and opens the way for the prophetic. The prophetic in turn prepares and opens the way for the teaching. Each one precedes and paves the way for the other. Each gift and ministry is designed by God in this way to open the way for the other to follow. Each territory needs all three to operate in order to establish God's purposes in that region.

Evangelism and pastoring are utilized as ways of reaching and overseeing the people. These gifts are important and necessary to perfect the saints and help fulfill the Great Commission. If the Church is apostolic, it will also be evangelistic in order to reach the lost; it will also be pastoral to protect and cover those who are saved. The apostolic cannot function without these two gifts and the others as well.

First Apostles

The Church of Jesus Christ is to be *first and foremost an apostolic Church*. This means it is to be chiefly, inherently, primarily and principally apostolic in character. This apostolic anointing was always intended to be the governing anointing of the Church. It governs, directs, sustains and motivates the Church toward the fulfillment of the Great Commission.

The apostolic gift and anointing should always be at the heart of the Church. It is the core, center and nucleus of what drives the Church—the central part around which the other parts are gathered and grouped. The early apostles provided the nucleus of the Church. Others began to gather around them, to function in their gifts and graces and to help them move toward fulfilling the Great Commission.

Apostleship, therefore, is a necessary and indispensable part of the Church. It is not optional, but needed and required. The Lord is raising up a company of apostolic people and churches that will be a core group around which others will gather and function.

When the apostolic becomes the principle anointing of the Church, it will set the tone for all that we do. It will cause the Church to be inclined toward fulfilling its commission. It will affect the personality, temperament and disposition of the Church. The Church will begin to have a certain flavor. This anointing will affect everything that we do, setting the tone for our prayer, worship, preaching, teaching and overall ministry. This was true in the book of Acts, and it is true today.

"Sing to Him a new song" (Ps. 33:3). We are to serve God in newness of spirit (see Rom. 7:6). To do that we must constantly receive fresh oil. This keeps the Church refreshed, renewed and restored. When the Church does not have this dynamic, it becomes dry, dull and stagnant. The Church loses its freshness and ultimately its appeal. Newness causes the Church to be attractive.

- "unshrunk [new] cloth on an old garment" (Matt. 9:16)
- "new wine into old wineskins" (Mark 2:22)
- "new things I declare" (Isa. 42:9)

New moves are apostolic. Someone has to initiate these new moves that have been prophetically spoken. That someone is the pioneer.

Pioneering Spirit

We have all benefited from pioneers. The Wright brothers were pioneers in aviation. The world has benefited greatly because of their vision. Alexander Graham Bell was a pioneer, and now we have global communications. Henry Ford was a pioneer, and now we don't have to drive around with a horse and buggy. The same is true in the areas of science, medicine, technology, literature and government.

America's founding fathers were pioneers. They fought a war, drew up a constitution and established the framework of the greatest republic in history. And who can forget all those movies and television programs vividly depicting brave pioneers in covered wagons, heading across the country through dangerous, unknown, even hostile territory? Carrying all their earthly belongings and dreams of a better life, these pioneers struggled forward, pushing on through heat-parched deserts and snowbound

THE APOSTOLIC ANOINTING KEEPS THE CHURCH FROM BEING OUTMODED AND OUTDATED. IT MAKES US RELEVANT TO OUR WORLD—WITHOUT COMPROMISE.

mountain ranges despite countless hardships, such as lack of water and food and constant threat of disease, injury and death. Yet without those hardy, persevering pioneers, much of this great country of ours would never have been settled.

Pioneers are often misunderstood, mistreated and misquoted.

The benefits of their lives are often seen only after they have passed from the scene. The early apostles were pioneers, laying the foundation for the Church and writing the New Testament. They left us with a heritage that has lasted 2,000 years. They were misunderstood and persecuted. And yet, because they were apostolic, they had the ability to overcome obstacles that would have stopped ordinary men.

Every generation and every age needs pioneers. Humans have a tendency to remain the same and sometimes even revert backward. Pioneers motivate and push us to go forward. They expand us and help us break through the barriers that would keep us from progressing. They stir us to do more, shake us from complacency and motivate us to reach a goal.

The apostolic anointing keeps us on the cutting edge. It pushes us forward toward the goal of fulfilling our commission. It releases us from the past and thrusts us into the future. It enables us to meet the challenges of a changing world. It keeps us from being outmoded and outdated. It makes us relevant to our world—without compromise. It keeps us advancing and improving.

Paul was a founder and a foundation layer. Apostles are founders. The early apostles laid the foundation of the Church (see 1 Cor. 3:10). Martin Luther laid the foundation for Reformation. John and Charles Wesley laid the foundation for the Methodist church. Every movement in the Church has had foundation layers. Every generation needs this kind of people. Without them, nothing is established for that generation. The apostolic spirit gives the ability to lay foundations for our generation. Without this dimension a whole generation can be lost.

Breakthrough Anointing

The commission that Jesus has given us demands that we penetrate every region and territory with the gospel. This requires a pioneering spirit and pioneering ability.

The early apostles had that pioneering spirit. They invaded new nations and territories with the gospel. They helped establish churches and pioneered new works. When a church does not have the apostolic anointing at its core, stagnation will result. Stagnation means not moving or flowing, showing no sign of activity or advancement. It means not developing or progressing. It means to come to a standstill, to abate, stop or cease.

The Church's progress is directly proportionate to the measure of apostolic grace operating within it at any given time. To pioneer means to advance, progress, gain ground or conquer territory. Pioneers and pioneering people will eventually succeed, flourish and prosper. Pioneers are usually men and women of extraordinary courage, talent, vision and ability. They are able to succeed in the face of overwhelming odds.

Frontiersmen, pathfinders, trailblazers, explorers, forerunners, innovators. Pioneers initiate, instigate, set in motion, trigger, start the ball rolling, take the first step, take the lead, break the ice, institute, inaugurate, found, establish, set up, lay the foundation, introduce, launch, usher in.

A pioneer is a catalyst. Pioneers cause things to happen. They do not sit back and wait for things to happen. They initiate new movements. They penetrate new territories. They preach new truths and birth new churches and ministries.

Our Lord Jesus was a pioneer. The early apostles were pioneers. This pioneering spirit has been in the Church throughout history. Martin Luther was a pioneer. John Wesley was a pioneer. Every move of God in the past has had pioneers.

How do we capture this pioneering spirit and keep it? Why do some get it only to lose it? If we understand what it is, we can better receive it, walk in it and keep it.

The pioneering spirit is apostolic. God always desires to do a new thing, and He will use apostolic people to do it. Apostolic people have the ability to persevere in the face of opposition. They have the strength and mentality of a pioneer. The apostolic anointing will set the tone for your life and ministry. You will become a pioneering believer. You will invade and possess new territory—naturally and spiritually.

Pioneers have a *breakthrough anointing*. The word "breakthrough" is defined as an act or instance of breaking through an obstruction; an offensive thrust that penetrates and carries beyond a defensive line in warfare.

Pioneers have the ability to break through ignorance, fear and other obstacles that keep people from advancing. Apostolic ministry has the ability to penetrate the defenses set up by the powers of darkness. This is why God has set it to be first. Someone must break through first before any significant progress can be made. Someone must have the courage, ability and power to *break through* the obstacles set up by the enemy.

Apostolic preaching and teaching has this penetrating power. There must be breakthroughs in finances, television, radio, publishing, building projects and other areas. We must be able to break through tradition, religion, ignorance, poverty, witchcraft, pride, rebellion and other obstacles. The apostle has the anointing to break through these things that people might be set free to walk in the truth.

Nations, cities and regions are opened up to the gospel because of this breakthrough anointing. Without this anointing, these areas will remain closed to the truth. This is why it is so difficult to break through in some cities, nations or groups of people. These areas and people need *sent ones*.

When apostles are sent into a region, they have the ability (through the anointing) to penetrate the darkness and bring light and revelation to the people. There is no substitute for the apostle. This ministry is like a battering ram against the citadels of the enemy.

Apostles are pathfinders. A pathfinder is one who discovers a way, especially one who explores untraversed regions to mark out a new route. Pioneers are the first to enter a new region. This can be a new region geographically or a new region of knowledge.

Pioneers leave a heritage for others to follow. They leave a spiritual legacy for those who will come after them. This ministry precedes and opens the way for others. The early apostles left a spiritual legacy for the Church to follow. We all have inherited the spiritual legacy of the early apostles.

A pioneer is also a frontiersman. Pioneers live and minister on the frontier. A frontier is a new field for developmental activity, a region that forms the margin of settled or developed territory. We call this "living on the cutting edge."

Often the Church becomes settled in a certain place. The Lord continues to send apostles to expand the Church's borders. They expand our spiritual horizons and release us from spiritual boundaries and limitations of tradition and past experience.

There is a song that we sing in our church, written by my good friend Kevin Leal. Following are the words to the chorus:

Opening places in the spirit
where men have never been.
Opening places in the spirit
so He can come again.
Opening places in the spirit
letting men break through.
Opening places in the spirit
touching you and you and you!

These are new places in the spirit that need to be opened where many saints have never been. It takes the anointing to open those places for others to follow and enter in. These are the individuals and churches that will operate in apostolic anointing to open new regions and new frontiers so that others may enter in and experience the fullness of God.

Opening New Regions to the Word of God

And the word of the Lord was being spread throughout all
the region (Acts 13:49).

Some believe their cities already have enough churches, and
they need to revive the existing ones rather than build new ones.
But many of the existing churches will not receive new things,
often fighting against a fresh move of the Holy Spirit. As a result,
many of the present churches are ineffective. This is why I do not
focus on the number of churches in an area, but on the number
of churches that are having an *impact*. Often the number ranges
from few to almost none.

This is why apostolic ministry is needed: to plant effective,
powerful churches that will have an impact!

Or how can one enter a strong man's house and plunder
his goods, unless he first binds the strong man? And then
he will plunder his house (Matt. 12:29).

Before a region opens to the gospel, however, the strongman
of Matthew 12:29 must first be bound. (See also Mark 3:27; Luke
11:21,22.) The strongman may in fact be a demonic principality
that rules over a certain geographical area, leading a horde of
demonic principalities that influence the affairs of people. The
Bible clearly demonstrates God's superiority over all these "principalities and powers." (Compare Daniel 7–10 with Ephesians
1:21 and 6:12, Colossians 1:16 and Romans 8:38, where the
Messiah decisively defeats all his enemies.) The "goods" are the
souls that are being influenced and controlled by this ruling spirit
to keep them from the truth. Apostles can go into new regions
and break through the resistance by binding the strongman.

The strongman is bound by the overall ministry of the apostle.

The apostle then establishes new churches and new revelation in these areas. Even where there are already churches in existence, an apostle can come in and establish new revelation. Often the strongmen in these areas are spirits of religion and tradition.

The apostle Paul had the desire to preach the gospel and to establish churches in new regions. He did not desire to boast in another man's work, but to preach Christ where He had not been preached (see 2 Cor. 10:16).

In addition to regions being opened up to the Word of God, the Lord uses apostles to affect cities as well (see Acts 13:44). Remember, some are called to cities, some to regions and some to nations. Those called to certain cities will be commissioned to establish the truth in that city. This does not mean that every church in that city comes under an apostle's authority. The apostle has authority only in the place where he ministers or is allowed to minister.

The Lord is now raising up apostles who will be voices in major cities. Wherever God sends His apostles, they will help change the spiritual climate of their assigned areas, whether those areas are cities, regions or nations. The result will be that the people in those areas are more receptive to hearing the Word of God—and the Church will be that much closer to fulfilling its mission.

CHAPTER FIVE

WARFARE

*For the weapons of our warfare are not carnal but
mighty in God for pulling down strongholds, casting
down arguments and every high thing that exalts itself
against the knowledge of God, bringing every thought
into captivity to the obedience of Christ.*

2 CORINTHIANS 10:4,5

Many Christians are familiar with these verses in 2 Corinthians,
and some are actively involved in practicing them. Yet countless
Christians lament their ineffectiveness when it comes to seeing
results in the area of spiritual warfare. Why is that?

The commission given to the Church requires us to invade
new territories—hostile territories. The powers of darkness that
have ruled regions for centuries will not give up without a fight.
They must be confronted, subdued and driven out. This requires
warfare.

Many do not understand the present-day emphasis in the
Church on spiritual warfare. Some even oppose the very thought
of it. But opposition notwithstanding, there is a growing emphasis today on warfare prayer. Dr. C. Peter Wagner of Global
Harvest Ministries in Colorado has written some excellent books
on warfare prayer called the *Prayer Warrior Series*, published by
Regal Books. I recommend these books highly to every pastor
and intercessor who wants a better understanding of this important subject.

Warfare is nothing new. The Bible is filled with warfare. Apostles and apostolic people will be a people of warfare, whether they use the term or not.

Pulling Down Strongholds

"Warfare" in 2 Corinthians 10:4 is translated from the Greek word *strateia*, meaning apostolic, career, military service (as one of hardship and danger). It is related to the Greek word *strateuomai*, meaning to execute the *apostolate* (with its arduous duties and functions) and to contend with carnal thoughts. Paul was saying that the weapons of his apostolic ministry were mighty for the pulling down of strongholds.

I am convinced that there are certain strongholds that cannot be destroyed without the apostolic anointing. "Stronghold" is the Greek word *ochuroma*, meaning a fortress, a castle, a fortified place. Satan and his demons have fortified themselves from invasion. They have built strongholds and fortified themselves in every region of the world to resist the advancement of the Kingdom. These strongholds must be dealt with if we are to see the fulfillment of the Great Commission. Apostles have the ability to confront and pull down these strongholds.

The apostle Paul links these strongholds with "imaginations." This is the Greek word *logismos*, meaning reasoning, thought, computation or logic. It carries the idea of holding something safely. It is simply the way people think based on their way of life, tradition, experience or past teaching. Unfortunately, most thinking is against the knowledge of God.

The stronghold is also made up of demonic influence. There is a wisdom that is earthly, sensual and devilish (see Jas. 3:15). *Logismos* can also be translated as "arguments." Strongholds are the mind-sets of people in a particular territory. These mind-sets are fortified places that keep out truth and hold in lies. Unbelievers have mind-sets that prevent them from receiving the truth of the gospel. Spiritual warfare involves demolishing these mind-sets so that people can receive and walk in the truth.

Dr. Clarence Walker defines a stronghold as a forceful, stubborn argument, rationale, opinion, idea and/or philosophy that is formed and resistant to the knowledge of Jesus Christ. The *Twentieth Century New Testament* translation says, "We are engaged in confuting arguments and pulling down every barrier raised against the knowledge of God." Strongholds do two things: They keep people from the knowledge of God, and they prevent people from obeying the truth. Ignorance and rebellion are the result.

The term *mind-set* depicts a combination of both mind and set. In other words, the mind is already settled on a set of beliefs, and therefore resistant to change. This means it is fixed and rigid. Most people who claim to be open-minded really are not. Their minds are closed and hardened to truth and revelation.

Mind-sets are the thought processes of people groups who have developed a way of thinking over centuries of time. It is a combination of their experiences and what they have been taught by their ancestors. Mind-sets are not easy to change. It takes a strong anointing to break through the defensive barriers in their minds and overcome the pride associated with their way of thinking.

People are proud of the way they think, even though it may be wrong. No one wants to admit they are wrong, particularly when their ancestors have thought a certain way for sometimes thousands of years. Humility must precede repentance, and pride will put up a fight.

These strongholds are so strong that they are likened to forts. A fort is a citadel, a garrison, a castle, a tower, a safeguard. We have all heard the saying, "Hold the fort!" It means to defend and maintain the status quo. People would rather maintain their present way of thinking than to change. They will defend the current way of thinking through argument and debate. They will contradict and even blaspheme if necessary.

Communism is a mind-set; it is an ideology and philosophy of life. Materialism is a mind-set that bases happiness on success. Islam is a mind-set. Hinduism is a mind-set. These philosophies control the minds of countless people. They are powerful strongholds that can only be overcome through apostolic preaching and teaching.

Strongholds are major hindrances to the advancement of the Church and must be dealt with apostolically. The preaching, teaching and overall ministry of apostolic people are weapons that are mighty through God for the pulling down of these strongholds. (Praise, worship and prayer also are effective weapons.) The first thing Jesus gave the Twelve when He sent them forth was power over devils (see Matt. 10:1).

The Church must have the ability to blast and demolish these fortresses. Apostolic ministry has the power and authority to destroy strongholds and change mind-sets. There is a grace, a supernatural ability to refute, disprove, discredit and expose these philosophies for what they are. People will not repent unless there is a change of mind. This is the warfare that the apostle Paul is referring to in 2 Corinthians 10:3-5—refuting arguments and taking captive philosophies that are contrary to the truth.

Greek Spirits

The Greek world in which the early apostles ministered was filled with such philosophies. The Greeks were lovers of wisdom. They were seekers of knowledge to the point of being guilty of mind idolatry. In other words, they worshiped knowledge. They were the guardians of Aristotle and Plato and countless other philosophers. They had strong opinions and defended their point of view. They took pleasure in arguing and debating.

It was into this kind of world the Church was birthed. It would have been impossible for the Church to succeed in its mission there without the grace of God. The apostolic grace and anointing upon the Early Church gave them the ability to challenge and overcome these strongholds.

We find these same spirits operating on many college campuses today. They are strongholds of intellectualism and rationalization. It is no coincidence that members of fraternities and sororities are called "Greeks." As I was traveling through a college town, the Spirit of the Lord drew my attention to the fraternity houses on the campus. As I looked at all of the Greek letters that identified the different fraternities and sororities, the words "Greek spirits" came into my spirit. As I meditated upon what the Holy Spirit gave me, I began to understand the kind of spirits that the early apostles encountered.

The world in their day was controlled politically by the Romans, but influenced culturally by the Greeks. Philosophy was a major stronghold. Spirits of intellectualism and rationalization prevented many from believing that Christ had risen from the dead. College campuses are filled with these kinds of spirits.

Spirits of intellectualism, rationalization, pride, debate and mind idolatry are ruling spirits in much of our education system. These are the same types of Greek spirits that the early apostles dealt with. Just as they were able to break through the arguments of pagan philosophy, so must we.

The *New English Bible* says, "We demolish sophistries and all that rears its proud head against the knowledge of God" (2 Cor. 10:5). Sophists were Greek philosophers who specialized in dialectic argumentation and rhetoric. They were professional philosophers and teachers skilled in elaborate and devious argumentation. Sophism today is defined as plausible but fallacious argument. In other words, it is deceptive. At the root of deceptive philosophy is the devil himself.

The Jews sought after a sign, and the Greeks sought after wisdom (see 1 Cor. 1:22). The Greeks, however, were not seeking after the wisdom of God. They were seeking after philosophy. Many viewed Christianity as just another philosophy open to debate. The

Phillips translation calls the type of wisdom sought by the Greeks "an intellectual panacea." They viewed philosophy and education as a cure-all. But we preach Christ crucified—to the Jews a stumbling block, to the Greeks foolishness (see 1 Cor. 1:23). The Greeks considered the preaching of the Cross to be nonsense.

It was into this pagan, Greek, philosophical world that the Early Church was thrust. They were carriers of an anointing that was able to pull down these strongholds. At the root of Greek philosophy was pride. The Greeks were proud of their philosophical heritage and argued when confronted with the truth of the gospel. Apostolic ministry confounds the philosophies of men. It is a ministry of power that breaks through the arguments that Satan has set up in the minds of men.

God uses this ministry to make foolish the wisdom of this world (see 1 Cor. 1:20). We need this same kind of ministry today to confront the arguments that our modern world raises against the truth. Although the arguments may have changed, the demonic influence behind them has not. We are dealing with ancient principalities that must be bound and cast out through apostolic ministry. These are stubborn arguments that refuse to budge; they can only be destroyed through apostolic ministry, an anointing that confounds the wisdom of this world and releases the wisdom of God.

The Church needs apostolic grace today to refute the arguments that people in our modern world use to reject the gospel. Miracles, healings, signs and wonders help to blast away these strongholds. People have no argument against the raw power of God. They have a difficult time explaining these things away. They are forced to rethink their positions and come face-to-face with the truth. Apostles come, not with enticing words of man's wisdom, but in demonstration of the Spirit and of power.

This is again why the Church must be, first and foremost, apostolic. Without this dimension, we will not have the ability to destroy these strongholds. We are not just dealing with views but

worldviews. Entire people groups think certain ways. Entire seg-
ments of the world think certain ways. Without the apostolic
anointing, how can we succeed against these pervasive worldviews?
How can we, without the apostolic anointing, free the millions of
people from mind-sets that will send them to eternal damnation?

The Apostle's Mantle

According to Dr. Paula A. Price in *God's Apostle Revived,* the apostle's mantle includes warfare strategy and rulership.[1] As mentioned
earlier, the Greek word *strateia* means military service or apostolic
career. The kin term *strateuomai* means to serve in a military cam-
paign, to execute the *apostolate.* This word's definition speaks of
armaments, troops and battle array. According to Dr. Price, the
apostle surfaces as an "arch warrior, a chief strategist, a competent
captain, and an able guard over his jurisdiction." His supernatural
rank in the *stratos* makes him a formidable combatant in the spirit realm and an arch rival to the forces in the heavenlies.

> Indeed I have given him as a witness to the people, a
> leader and commander for the people (Isa. 55:4).

Although every believer has rank to cast out devils, apostles
walk and minister in the highest rank. Evil spirits and angels recognize this rank. Apostles are the spiritual commanders of the
Church. "Commander," as used in Isaiah 55:4, is the Hebrew word
tsavah, meaning to command, send a message, to put or set in order.
The Church needs apostolic leadership to help set the Church in
order. They help organize and mobilize the believers into an army.

Apostles are standard-bearers—commanders who lift the
standard and rally the army of God (see Isa. 59:19). An apostolic
church is a church that is awesome or terrible, as an army with
banners (see Song of Sol. 6:4,10). Apostolic churches strike fear
into the kingdom of darkness.

Apostles have the ability as generals and commanders to mobilize the saints for war. Apostles rally the people of God. To rally means to bring to order again, to gather and organize anew. It is the ability to draw people together for action. Apostles are endued with the rank and authority to do this. They are leaders with the necessary grace, charisma and wisdom to lead the Church.

 ## APOSTOLIC CHURCHES STRIKE FEAR INTO THE KINGDOM OF DARKNESS.

Apostolic ministry is a ministry of warfare. It entails commanding, mobilizing, rallying and gathering the army of God to challenge and pull down the strongholds of the enemy. The apostolic invades new territories and breaks through. It has the ability to go first. It is the first to encounter the spiritual resistance of the powers of darkness and the first to penetrate the barriers they erect. This ministry is absolutely necessary to keep the Church advancing toward the completion of the Great Commission.

The Ravenous Bird

Declaring the end from the beginning, and from ancient times things that are not yet done, saying, "My counsel shall stand, and I will do all My pleasure," calling a [ravenous] bird of prey from the east, the man who executes My counsel, from a far country. Indeed I have spoken it; I will also bring it to pass. I have purposed it; I will also do it (Isa. 46:10,11).

God has a plan and purpose He will fulfill. It has already been spoken by the prophets. Nothing will stand in the way of His fulfilling His good pleasure; His counsel shall stand. We have the glorious opportunity of being a part of this plan. As we discover the plan of God, we pray and align ourselves with His will. We are laborers together with God.

God calls the ravenous bird of prey to execute His purposes. This is a prophetic symbol of the apostolic ministry. The ravenous bird is the Hebrew word *ayit*, meaning a hawk. It also means to swoop down upon. The hawk is a symbol of war, representing the militaristic aspect of the apostle's mantle.

Another contemporary definition for "hawk" is one who demonstrates an actively aggressive or combative attitude. It is a person who favors military force or action in order to carry out a foreign policy. What a symbol for the apostolic!

The Church also has a foreign policy. We are commissioned to go into all the world and preach the gospel. We must have an aggressive, warlike attitude against the forces of darkness that would attempt to stop us.

The hawk symbolizes sharpness, keen vision and quickness. It represents discernment and insight into the plans and purposes of God. The hawk is a swift bird that suddenly seizes its prey. It is a ravenous bird. Ravenous means extremely hungry, voracious or greedy for gratification. This bird symbolizes the militant, aggressive and warlike aspect of the apostolic ministry. It is needed to execute the plans of God.

As an officer in the Church, the apostle is also an executive. He is a person who executes power in the Church. In other words, he has the power and authority to execute the plans and purposes of God. To execute means to put into effect, to carry out, to perform, to fulfill, to finish. The purposes of God will not be fulfilled or carried out without the apostolic ministry being restored to the Church.

For too long the Church has tried to carry out the plan of God while ignoring this vital ministry. God calls the ravenous bird to execute His counsel. These are military generals and commanders who will mobilize the people of God for the fulfillment of God's purposes. They have an appetite and an authority to execute. We need people who do more than talk and sing. They must *do* and *act*. They have the ability to finish and complete the commissions given to them by the Lord.

The apostolic Church must be quick in executing the plans of the Lord. The hawk moves swiftly; it does not take long to swoop down upon and devour its prey. The Church in the book of Acts experienced rapid movement, achieving tremendous breakthroughs in a short period of time. The move of God accelerated and gained momentum from Jerusalem on the day of Pentecost. Large numbers of believers were added to the Church quickly. This is the kind of anointing the Church will need in the last days to fulfill the Great Commission. There is much work to be done in a short period. The Lord desires to do a quick work.

Prayer and the Apostolic

Therefore pray the Lord of the harvest to send out laborers into His harvest (Matt. 9:38).

We are living in the midst of the greatest prayer revival the world has ever known. More people are praying for revival and global evangelism than ever before. Recent breakthroughs in the 10/40 window—the geographical area between 10° and 40° north of the equator, ranging from west Africa to the Far East—have been attributed to this recent prayer movement. Prayer teams are visiting remote and isolated places to pray for the fulfillment of the Great Commission. Gateway cities are being targeted for prayer in nations with little or no Christian presence. God is stirring His people to pray around the world. What is happening? Is this the sign that we may be nearing the final thrust in world evangelization? I believe the answer is *yes*.

The worldwide prayer movement is releasing an apostolic spirit upon the Church. This is because *prayer releases the apos-*

tolic anointing. Jesus encouraged us to pray to the Lord to send forth laborers into His harvest (see Luke 10:2). Remember, *send forth* is an apostolic term. This shows us the connection between prayer and the apostolic.

The apostolic revolves around the concept of sending and being sent. God has always been a *sending* God. He sent Moses into Egypt when He heard the cries of His people in bondage. He continually sent prophets to Israel to warn them of the consequences of their rebellion. He sent John the Baptist to prepare the way of the Lord. He sent His only begotten Son to die for the sins of the world. He sent the Holy Spirit to help us and to be our Comforter. The apostolic spirit is a part of the very nature of God.

Our prayers move God. He responds to our prayers by sending forth His Spirit. He sends laborers as a result of our prayers. This is why the Lord encourages us to pray. Every nation needs sent ones. The harvest is plenteous, but the laborers are few. The world needs apostolic laborers to bring in the harvest.

I believe that, in response to the millions who are currently praying, more apostles and apostolic ministries will be released in this hour than ever before. In fact, I believe the greatest apostolic spirit the world has ever known is even now beginning to be released. It will be greater than what we read of in the book of Acts. The coming move of God will dwarf the acts of the apostles by comparison. It is already happening. The largest churches the world has ever known are now on the earth. There are more Christians alive today than at any other time in history. There are more miracles and healings taking place than ever before. There are more apostles and prophets on the earth than ever before. We are living in apostolic times.

Apostolic Times

Behold, you despisers, marvel and perish! For I work a work in your days, a work which you will by no means believe, though one were to declare it to you (Acts 13:41).

Look among the nations and watch—Be utterly astounded! For I will work a work in your days which you would not believe, though it were told you (Hab. 1:5).

Paul quoted the prophecy of Habakkuk in describing what was taking place in the book of Acts. It was a warning to the Jews who would not believe the numbers of Gentiles that God would receive by their faith. It was something so new and awesome that there was a danger of despising it. Habakkuk told them to look out among the heathen and wonder. God was about to do something in the nations of the world that would be unbelievable.

This verse describes what takes place during apostolic times. No one would doubt that the book of Acts describes what took place during apostolic times. What Habakkuk stated, however, can happen at any time—and it is happening today. God is working in the nations of the world. We are looking out among the nations and seeing what we may not have believed several years ago. This is why I say we are now living in apostolic times.

Apostolic times are seasons in which God releases an apostolic spirit to the Church. God begins to raise up apostolic leaders and apostolic churches. This is always in response to prayer, and this is what is happening today. Apostles are being positioned in every nation to reap an end-times harvest.

Praying with Power

Now it came to pass in those days that He went out to the mountain to pray, and continued all night in prayer to God. And when it was day, He called His disciples to Himself; and from them He chose twelve whom He also named apostles (Luke 6:12,13).

Notice Jesus prayed all night before choosing the Twelve. Again, prayer releases the apostolic. I encourage churches to pray for their cities and nations to release an apostolic spirit into that region. Our local church in Chicago has emphasized all-night prayer to release the apostolic spirit into our own region. All-night prayer is a powerful way to release the apostolic spirit.

As we pray, apostles can be identified and released into every region. We need to identify the true apostles in a region. They may not be the ones *we* would identify; we need to know whom *God* identifies. A well-known preacher may not be the one. Sometimes those whom God chooses are hidden until prayer releases them.

Prayer not only releases the apostolic spirit; it sustains an apostolic movement. Prayer releases spiritual impetus and momentum. The Church in the book of Acts was a praying church. They continued to break through in spite of resistance, persecution, even death. They prayed until "the place where they were assembled together was shaken" (Acts 4:31). The result of their praying was an apostolic release of great power and great grace (see v. 33). Signs and wonders were released, and "believers were increasingly added to the Lord" (Acts 5:14). The apostolic spirit that is released through prayer fuels church growth; it is a harvest anointing.

The apostles gave themselves continually to prayer (see Acts 6:4). Prayer is the strength of the apostolic ministry. Apostolic churches are being raised up throughout the earth that will be houses of prayer for all nations (see Isa. 56:7); then we can ask God for the nations (see Ps. 2:8).

Because of the authority and power resident within the apostolic anointing, greater results take place when we pray apostolically. Many have heard of prophetic prayer, but few have heard of apostolic prayer.

Apostolic prayer is strategic prayer. It is a governmental praying. It is global in perspective, with a wisdom to fulfill God's end-times purposes. This is because apostles, along with prophets, bring revelation to the Church to fulfill the plans and purposes of the Lord. They give us insight into the eternal purposes of God. Those who come into contact with true apostles gain a better understanding of God's purposes as revealed in the Word of God.

Apostolic prayer is revelational. Apostolic people pray with the advantage of the wisdom of God. It is praying with the authority that comes from revelation. We are praying things today that we never prayed five years ago. This is because we are seeing things in the Word we never saw before. As a result, our prayers are stronger and deeper than ever before.

Apostolic prayer is warfare prayer. Epaphras labored fervently in prayer for the Colossian church (see Col. 4:12). *Laboring* is an apostolic term. It is the Greek word *agonizomia*, meaning to struggle or contend with an adversary, to strive. Apostles and apostolic people contend with the powers of darkness in prayer. Apostolic prayer breaks the resistance in regions that have been held captive by the powers of darkness. This type of intercession will help believers stand perfect and complete in all the will of God.

Apostolic prayer is unceasing (see 1 Thess. 5:17). It does not rest until the plans and purposes of God are complete. The apostolic ministry is tenacious and relentless in its drive to finish. It does not cease because of resistance or temporary setbacks. It continues to pioneer and break through every barrier until the commission is fulfilled. This is another reason Satan hates and fears this anointing. It is an unstoppable force. It is persistent and patient in spite of trials and tribulations. It is a battering ram against the citadels of darkness.

The Antioch Principle

Now in the church that was at Antioch there were certain prophets and teachers: Barnabas, Simeon who was called Niger, Lucius of Cyrene, Manaen who had been brought up with Herod the tetrarch, and Saul. As they ministered to the Lord and fasted, the Holy Spirit said, "Now separate to Me Barnabas and Saul for the work to which I have called them."

Then, having fasted and prayed, and laid hands on them, they sent them away. So, being sent out by the Holy Spirit,

they went down to Seleucia, and from there they sailed to
Cyprus (Acts 13:1-4).

Apostolic times are times in which the apostolic spirit and the
apostolic ministry are being released. This can be done through
prayer; it is happening today. There is, however, another way to
release the apostolic. I call this the "Antioch principle." It is
based on what happened in the church at Antioch. As the
prophets and teachers came together to minister to the Lord and
fast, the Holy Ghost said, "Separate to Me Barnabas and Saul."
They were separated for an apostolic ministry. Ministering to the
Lord and fasting helped release them into their ministries.

There is also in these verses a prophetic element for the
Church today. The Scripture identifies prophets and teachers
coming together to minister to the Lord and to fast. I believe this
represents the two movements that preceded this present apostolic move. The Church has already seen a release of the teaching
anointing and the prophetic anointing. It is important that these
two movements come together to help release the apostolic
anointing. Prophets and teachers should not fight apostles, but
rather be a part of releasing them. Some of the prophets and
teachers themselves will be released into apostolic ministries.

Fasting, along with prayer, is a way of releasing apostles. After
the church of Antioch fasted and prayed, they sent Barnabas and
Saul away. These two apostles were released through fasting and
praying. They were then sent forth by the Holy Spirit.

A Finishing Anointing

Jesus said to them, "My food is to do the will of Him who
sent Me, and to finish His work" (John 4:34).

Notice the two words "sent" and "finish." Jesus was *sent* by the Father,
and His desire was to *finish* His mission. This verse connects being

sent with finishing. This is why I call the apostolic anointing a "finishing anointing." It will take an apostolic Church to finish the Great Commission. To finish not only means to reach the end of a task or course, it means something that completes, concludes or perfects.

The Lord is preparing the Church to complete its task, and the apostolic ministry is absolutely essential to prepare the Church for this purpose. Without the ministry of the apostle, the Church will lack the necessary grace, power and authority to finish or complete its mission.

> And see, now I go bound in the spirit to Jerusalem, not knowing the things that will happen to me there, except that the Holy Spirit testifies in every city, saying that chains and tribulations await me.
>
> But none of these things move me; nor do I count my life dear to myself, so that I may finish my race with joy, and the ministry which I received from the Lord Jesus, to testify to the gospel of the grace of God (Acts 20:22-24).

Notice Paul's attitude. He was determined to finish his course. Nothing could dissuade him from completing his ministry. There was a drive and a determination to finish. This must be the mind-set of the Church today. We must have an apostolic mind-set; we must be driven and determined to complete the Great Commission. This mind-set overcomes all obstacles and hindrances that stand in the way of finishing.

Trials, tests and tribulations do not deter the true apostolic ministry. There is a grace resident within this anointing that overcomes all opposition and breaks through every barrier. And it does not cease until the task is complete.

Note

1. Paula A. Price, *God's Apostle Revived* (Everlasting Life Publications: Plainfield, New Jersey, 1994).

CHAPTER SIX

APOSTOLIC REFORMATION

The Church is now experiencing another reformation, and that means God is working changes in His people—changes that affect every area of our lives, particularly in the way we think, or our *mind-sets*. Change is uncomfortable but necessary. Reformation is a radical process involving amendment, correction, rectification, renovation, reclamation, recovery, salvation, rescue and deliverance. The Church—and all who are part of it—at one time or another must experience all these.

A time of reformation is a season of revolutionary change. It is not the season for the fearful and fainthearted. It is the season for the boldness of the apostolic anointing to come forth. Apostles boldly challenge the status quo and force change for the better. They are not concerned with changing the Church for the sake of change; they are concerned with the condition of the Church. They are sent to correct things that are not in line with God's purpose for His Church.

The apostolic anointing helps to keep the Church current and relevant with each changing generation, without compromise. Outdated and outmoded ways of ministry must be changed in order to effectively touch each new generation. The spirit of reformation is the spirit of change. It contains the new thing that the Lord is doing in any given era. Reformation blesses and strengthens the Church and keeps the Church moving toward the fulfillment of the Great Commission.

Whenever there is a need for reformation, the Lord sends forth apostles. Apostles have the ability to pull down the strongholds of tradition and bring forth new revelation. Apostles operate and minister under a reforming anointing. When the Church is out of order and not in proper form, there is a need to *re-form*. Apostles have the discernment to know when the Church is not in its proper form.

The Spirit of the Reformer

> And if by these things you are not reformed by Me, but walk contrary to Me, then I also will walk contrary to you, and I will punish you yet seven times for your sins (Lev. 26:23,24).

Reformation is not new. Even the Protestant Reformation of the sixteenth century was not the first reformation for the people of God. The Lord spoke of reformation as early as the book of Leviticus. The beginning of the New Covenant through the apostles was also a time of reformation. The Lord is always concerned about the shape and form of His Church.

One of the functions of the apostle is to bring the Church into proper form. Apostles are concerned with biblical order. If the Church is not in the correct form, the apostle will come in the spirit of the reformer. God will send apostles to bring reformation to the Church.

> Concerned only with foods and drinks, various washings, and fleshly ordinances imposed until the time of *reformation* (Heb. 9:10, italics added).

There are times of reformation that are *predestined* by the Lord. There is also a release of the apostolic anointing to bring about the changes *ordained* by the Lord.

Religious systems that have been in place for years prior to a reformation are the greatest enemies to a new move of God. Religious systems that need reform serve the interests of the leadership of that system, and they are usually a reformation's greatest opponents. During the days of Jesus and the early apostles, the Sadducees and Pharisees had much to lose in a reformation: their position, power and control over the people. The early apostles were persecuted by these leaders in order to prevent the completion of a reformation.

Apostolic Boldness

And when they had prayed, the place where they were assembled together was shaken; and they were all filled with the Holy Spirit, and they spoke the word of God with boldness (Acts 4:31).

In the midst of persecution comes apostolic boldness. Apostolic reformers are noted for their boldness in preaching the truth in spite of persecution and even death. Intimidation is a tool of the devil to stop reformation. The enemy does not want the Church to come into the form intended by the Lord. When the Church comes into proper form, it will fulfill the plan of God in the earth. Until then, the enemy will use every method at his disposal to stop reformation, but one of his major weapons is intimidation.

Now, Lord, look on their threats, and grant to Your servants that with all boldness they may speak Your word (Acts 4:29).

Religious systems and leaders who desire to maintain the status quo for their own benefit will use threats against apostolic reformers. But apostolic reformers have the anointing and boldness to bring about reform in the face of staunch opposition. They are hated and called troublemakers because of their message, but they bring to the Church what it needs most—reformation!

The Lion-Hearted Reformer

Martin Luther was called the lion-hearted reformer because of his boldness and stand against the errors of the institutional Church of his day. His ministry was apostolic, and he is a prime example of an apostolic reformer.

In 1517, Pope Leo X needed money to finish building St. Peter's Church in Rome. He granted permission to a man named John Tetzel, a dominican monk, to sell indulgences to finance the building of the cathedral. An indulgence was a promise to the buyer, granted by the pope, of a reduction of length of stay in purgatory (according to Roman Catholic doctrine, the place a believer goes after death to be purged from sins and made ready for heaven). It was an official pardon from the Church, granted for a certain amount of money, which was in turn used to finance the building of St. Peter's.

The Catholic Church was in essence *selling* forgiveness of sin. This was, of course, nonscriptural, but the majority of the people believed what they were taught by the Church. The Scriptures were interpreted by the clergy, who in turn were bound by an oath to follow the teachings of the Church and the pope, who was considered infallible.

When Martin Luther, who at the time was an Augustinian monk committed to the Church, heard of Tetzel selling pardons, he posted 95 theses, or statements, to a church door in Wittenburg, Germany, opposing the buying and selling of pardons.

Luther was not trying to leave the Church by posting his 95 theses, but was acting as a scholar desiring to debate the subject. In his day, if a scholar wanted to debate on a subject, it was proper to write the arguments out and post them in a public place. In this case, Luther nailed his 95 arguments on a church door on October 31, 1517.

He had no idea his 95 theses would cause such an uproar in the Church. His statements were translated from Latin to German and circulated among the common people. Soon Tetzel began having trouble selling indulgences and began to attack Luther, accusing him of being a traitor to the Church. Luther was summoned to Rome to answer these charges. He feared for his life, knowing that many who had attacked or questioned the teachings of the Church had been burned at the stake for heresy.

Luther instead went to Augsburg, Germany, to be interviewed by a cardinal named Cajetan, who requested Luther apologize for his 95 theses. However, Luther refused and ended up fleeing Augsburg.

On June 15, 1520, Leo X gave Luther 60 days to take back everything he had written or be excommunicated from the Church. By the time Luther received this ultimatum, four months had passed, and his writings were being burned in Rome and many cities in Germany by order of the pope. In some cities, however, the people refused to burn his writings, and instead defended him.

The Church was losing its grip on the minds of many of the people who had been exposed to Luther's writings. In Wittenburg on December 10, 1520, Luther responded by burning the most sacred writings of the Church, including the pope's order. Martin Luther was excommunicated from the Church on January 3, 1521.

Martin Luther's simple act of nailing his 95 theses on a church door began what is know as the Protestant Reformation. The spirit of reformation was upon him as he began to attack the teachings of the Church that were not based on the Word of God. He began translating the Scriptures from Latin to German for the common people to read and understand. People in many cities began to destroy statues, and priests began to marry.

Those who followed the reforms were called Lutherans. The Roman Church, concerned with stemming the tide of Lutheranism, called upon the German princes to seize Luther, but there were many who supported him, and some feared the social unrest that would occur if they obeyed the pope's edict.

Luther began teaching and training pastors and preachers, many of whom knew nothing of the Word of God. Whenever there is reform, there must also be a retraining of ministers to

THE APOSTOLIC ANOINTING UPON MARTIN LUTHER WAS STRONG ENOUGH TO SHAKE THE ENTIRE RELIGIOUS SYSTEM OF HIS DAY.

maintain the new form of the Church brought about by the reform. Apostles also train people with other ministry gifts (such as pastors and teachers) to sustain and carry on what reformation has begun. Luther also published books of his sermons for preachers to read and study.

Luther was not the only apostolic reformer of his day, but he is often referred to as "the father of the Reformation." The apostolic anointing that was upon Martin Luther was strong enough to shake the entire religious system of his day. The form of the Church during his day was not correct because it was not based on the Word of God. Luther caused the people to return *to* the Scriptures and *away* from the traditions of men. Apostles have the ability to steer the Church in the right direction. This is one of the reasons we need apostles today.

The Church has always needed apostles, because it has a tendency to be influenced by the traditions of men and stray from the course ordained by God. Reformation is unpleasant and controversial but absolutely necessary. The Lord will continue to reform the Church until it is the glorious Church prophesied in the Word of God. He will continue to raise up and use apostles to accomplish His purpose for the Church in the days ahead.

The Defense and Confirmation of the Gospel

Soon after I taught in our city a series on the subject of curses, there came forth some ministries attacking the idea that many believers have curses over their lives that need to be broken. I had been teaching this series for a month and was seeing tremendous results. Many believers were being set free from curses and from the demons operating behind the curses. Nevertheless, there are many who teach that Christians don't need deliverance from demons.

We have dealt with this opposition before and will continue to do so. However, this time an anger rose up in me to defend the truth: *Christians need deliverance* from curses and demons. The Lord was telling me that *truth must be defended*. It was through a member of our church that the Lord called my attention to the words of Paul in the first chapter of Philippians.

Just as it is right for me to think this of you all, because I have you in my heart, inasmuch as both in my chains and in the *defense* and confirmation of the gospel, you all are partakers with me of grace (Phil. 1:7, italics added).

Or out *defending* and vindicating the good news (Phil. 1:7, WNT, italics added).

Paul later said, "I am appointed for the *defense* of the gospel" (Phil. 1:17). As we continue to seek the Lord concerning the ministry of the apostle, we are receiving more revelation about the purpose and function of this office. One of the job descriptions of the apostle is *defender of the faith*.

There is an anointing that comes upon apostles to defend the truth. When the truth is attacked, there is an ability to confront opposition with the two-edged sword of the Word of God coming out of the apostle's mouth. When the truth is attacked, the anointing upon the apostle will quiet and confront those who attack the truth.

The apostolic anointing is at times confrontational. Apostles will not, however, confront out of hurt or bitterness, but out of a desire to protect and defend the truth.

> But when I saw that they were not straightforward about the truth of the gospel, I said to Peter before them all, "If you, being a Jew, live in the manner of Gentiles and not as the Jews, why do you compel Gentiles to live as Jews?" (Gal. 2:14).

When people don't walk according to the truth, the apostle will confront and correct them. Here we see the apostle Paul rebuking and confronting Peter because he was not walking uprightly according to the truth. Paul was defending the *truth*. There are those who believe apostles to be troublemakers because they are confrontational. Some would say, "Let's overlook certain discrepancies for the sake of peace." But apostolic ministry does not see things this way.

Truth cannot be compromised for the sake of peace. The truth *will* bring division. A man's foes will be those of his own household. Jesus said, "I did not come to bring peace but a sword" (Matt. 10:34). Truth is the sharp two-edged sword of God's Word that will cause division. Truth separates and divides (see Heb. 4:12).

Thus the apostle's preaching and teaching is often confrontational. Apostles confront the false doctrines and teachings of men. They also confront tradition when it has made the Word of God of no effect. Truth must be *preached, defended* and *confirmed*. The Lord will confirm the Word (truth) with signs following (see Mark 16:20).

Signs and wonders will follow the preaching and teaching of apostles, because God confirms the truth that apostles present. Although men may oppose their words, God will back them up.

Apostles are sent by God, and He puts a word of truth in their mouths.

Paul preached the gospel of the grace of God. His gospel was grace *without* the works of the law. He had to defend this truth from those who preached Christ *plus* the works of the law.

To whom we did not yield submission even for an hour, that *the truth of the gospel might continue with you* (Gal. 2:5, italics added).

True apostolic ministry will not budge when it comes to the truth. The Phillips translation says, "We did not give those men an inch."

True apostles *won't* give an inch. I call this an "apostolic stand." Apostles take a stand when it comes to the truth, and they defend it! Their major concern is that the Church continue in truth.

When apostolic anointing is lacking or absent, the Church can easily be led astray from the truth into error. The apostolic anointing serves as a buttress against error. This is why the enemy hates it and fights it so viciously. He must get the apostles out of the way in order to lead the Church into error. He will try to neutralize apostles or destroy them, if possible.

Paul defended the truth of the gospel against those who were attempting to oppose the message he preached. They were trying to mix law and grace. Paul refused to yield to them so that the truth would be maintained for the Church.

Apostles are set for the defense of the gospel. True apostles are defenders of the faith. They deliver God's people from the evil attacks of those who oppose the truth. Apostles have a zeal to guard and protect the truth, and there is an apostolic anger that will come forth when the truth is attacked.

All attacks do not come from outside the Church, however. We aren't surprised when atheists, humanists and liberals attack the Word of God. This is to be expected. But there are also attacks that come from within the Body. There are churches and believers who attack the truth of healing, deliverance, the baptism of the Holy Spirit, prophetic ministry and apostolic ministry.

The Lord is raising up apostles to defend and confirm the truth. This is to deliver the saints from succumbing to the attacks of those who resist the truth, to keep the Church walking in the truth and to continue in the Word.

> And after Abimelech there arose to defend Israel Tola the son of Puah, the son of Dodo, a man of Issachar (Judg. 10:1, *KJV*).

Like Tola, who defended Israel, apostles defend truth. Knox's translation calls Tola "the next champion." Tola is a type of apostolic ministry. He defended and delivered Israel from the enemy.

To defend means to drive back danger or attack; to maintain or support in the face of argument or hostile criticism; to prove valid; to take action against a challenge. It means to defend, protect, shield and safeguard.

The truth must be defended. That means the truth of the gospel must be defended. The gospel is the good news that Jesus saves from sin, sickness, curses, demons and hell. It is the full gospel of deliverance from all the results of Adam's transgression.

> And after him was Shammah the son of Agee the Hararite. The Philistines had gathered together into a troop where there was a piece of ground full of lentils. So the people fled from the Philistines.
>
> But he stationed himself in the middle of the field, defended it, and killed the Philistines. So the Lord brought about a great victory (2 Sam. 23:11,12).

Shammah *positioned* himself in the middle of the field and *defended* it. We need to position ourselves to defend the truth.

Paul said he was set for the *defense of the gospel*. Shammah did not back down and run even though all the others did. This must be our attitude: *If everyone else runs, I will stand my ground and defend the truth.*

The Lord can use one person who stands more than 99 who run. Our posture must be *to stand*. Someone must stand when the truth is under attack. Someone must speak out. Someone must challenge false teaching when it tries to invade the Church.

Modern-day Pharisees, scribes and religious leaders can gather together against the truth. Apostles are fearless and will rise up to meet the challenge. They will drive danger and attack away from the Church. Their preaching and teaching may become violent and polemic. But they will minister out of a boldness to preach truth in spite of the consequences.

Polemic Preaching

During the reformation of the sixteenth century, Martin Luther and other reformers were known for their polemic preaching and writing. Polemic means an aggressive attack on, or refutation of, the opinions or principles of another. It is the art or practice of disputation or controversy.

The word is derived from the Greek word *polemikos*, meaning warlike or hostile. The reformers aggressively attacked the error and hypocrisy of the established Church, and defended the truth of the gospel against those who attacked their teachings. Their major concern was that the truth be preached and taught at any cost. They would die for the truth; truth was the only thing that mattered.

Today's Church knows little about polemic preaching and writing. If one stands up for the truth of what he or she believes, that person is labeled dogmatic and non-ecumenical. The spirit of compromise has entered many churches, and they are not as concerned about the truth. But the Lord has always raised up defenders of the faith, people who are not afraid to preach and defend the truth. They recognize that the truth must not only be preached, but defended. If men do not defend the truth, lies will prevail. If lies prevail, people walk in bondage and deception. This is another reason why the Church needs the ministry of the apostle.

Apostles have an anointing to defend and confirm the truth. They walk in boldness and proclaim the truth in spite of persecution and opposition. The Lord puts a word in their mouths to confound adversaries or opponents, or as the *King James Version* calls them, the "gainsayers." To gainsay means to deny, dispute, contradict and oppose.

For I will give you a mouth and wisdom, which all your adversaries shall not be able to gainsay nor resist (Luke 21:15, *KJV*).

The Williams translation says, "All your opponents combined will not be able to resist and refute."

According to Titus 1:9, a bishop—overseer, pastor—should "by sound doctrine" both "exhort" and "convince" the gainsayers (*KJV*). This Scripture goes on to say:

For there are many insubordinate, both idle talkers and deceivers, especially those of the circumcision, whose *mouths must be stopped*, who subvert whole households, teaching things which they ought not, for the sake of dishonest gain (Titus 1:10,11, *NKJV*, italics added).

The Word of God says that there are mouths that must be stopped. The only way to stop some mouths is through polemic preaching, "sound speech that cannot be condemned, that one who is an opponent may be ashamed, having nothing evil to say of you" (Titus 2:8).

The Beck translation says, "so that anyone who opposes us will feel foolish." The Norlie translation says, "Your message should be true, your language correct and not open to criticism. In that way, your opponent may be put to shame."

The art of the polemic is speaking the right words with apostolic wisdom to put to shame those that oppose the truth. "How forceful are right words" (Job 6:25). The correct argument, using the right words, carries tremendous force. This is not the wishy-washy Christianity that we see so much of today. This is a return to *apostolic* Christianity.

And this is what the Lord is restoring to the Church. Don't let it surprise or confuse you. It is necessary for the Church to continue to walk in the truth. The Lord is raising up apostles whose words will shake the Church. Their words will be as a bulldozer in the spirit plowing through the lies the enemy has sown in the Church. As a result, the truth will prevail, and multitudes will be set free.

THE APOSTOLIC SEAL

*Even if I am not considered an apostle (a special
messenger) by others, at least I am one to you; for you
are the seal (the certificate, the living evidence) of
my apostleship in the Lord [confirming and
authenticating it].*

1 C O R I N T H I A N S 9 : 2 , *A M P L I F I E D*

The apostle Paul referred to those who had become believers
through his ministry as "epistles of Christ." His description of
these converts also applies to believers today:

You are our epistle written in our hearts, known and read
by all men; clearly you are an epistle of Christ, ministered
by us, written not with ink but by the Spirit of the living
God, not on tablets of stone but on tablets of flesh, that is,
of the heart (2 Cor. 3:2,3).

All of us who believe on Jesus Christ as Lord and Savior are
epistles of Christ. What does that mean? It means that believers
and unbelievers alike look upon us and "read" the gospel by the
way we live our lives. And the way we live our lives—the witness
we give to those who watch us—reflects the apostolic ministry
that birthed and/or discipled us.

This is an awesome responsibility, not only for apostles, but for all believers. If we want to be epistles that positively affect the lives of those who "read" us, we need to reflect an apostolic dimension in our lives that will lift up the name of Jesus and draw all men to Him (see John 12:32).

The *apostolic seal* is the visible sign, mark or symbol that serves as evidence of a true apostolic ministry. The seal of a true apostle will be the people (believers) birthed and raised up through the apostle's ministry. These believers will have an apostolic dimension in their lives because of the gifting of the apostle; they will have an apostle's stamp upon them. They will be an apostolic company of believers, the visible evidence of a true apostle's calling. And they will manifest the characteristics of an apostolic ministry.

A seal is an embossed emblem, symbol or letter that serves as evidence of authenticity. It is an authenticating mark or symbol that establishes something or someone as genuine. The apostolic seal authenticates the ministry of a true apostle. This seal or stamp will be upon the believers who are a product of the apostle's ministry.

Identifying True Apostles

Let's take a look at the distinguishing marks of an apostolic ministry. False apostles will not have this seal. Neither they nor their followers will bear these distinguishing marks. It is important to recognize the apostolic seal, because it can be used to authenticate, to distinguish the false from the true.

> And you have tested those who say they are apostles and are not, and have found them liars (Rev. 2:2).

We are to test or try those who say they are apostles. The church at Ephesus was commended by the Lord for testing those who claimed to be apostles. The Berkeley version says, "How you have put to the test those who call themselves apostles though *they are not*, and you have found them to be impostors" (*MLB*, italics added).

We are to test or prove all things (see 1 Thess. 5:21). It is important that we know the characteristics of true apostles so we can approve and be blessed by their ministries. There are many who claim apostleship but do not have the grace to walk in this office. "For such are false apostles, deceitful workers, transforming themselves into apostles of Christ" (2 Cor. 11:13).

We must keep in mind that there is a difference between standing in the office of an apostle and being apostolic. Every believer and minister can and should be apostolic to some degree. The Holy Spirit is an apostolic Spirit, and He dwells in all believers. Likewise, every church should have an apostolic dimension. But there are those pastors who mistakenly identify themselves as apostles because, to some degree, they have an apostolic dimension operating in their ministries. It is unwise and dangerous to try to walk in an office in which we are not graced to operate.

There are some definite characteristics of true apostles. Roger Sapp, in his book *The Last Apostles on Earth*, lists five characteristics of true apostles:

1. *Signs, Wonders, and Miracles* (2 Cor. 12:12). The preaching of the apostle must be accompanied by deliverance from evil spirits, healing the sick and miracles. Clearly this mark is not enough to establish the apostleship of a particular servant of God, but it is the first characteristic that every apostolic ministry will have.
2. *Revelation of the Calling to Independent Witnesses* (Acts 13:1,2). When an apostle is prepared to function in this calling, God will reveal this to independent witnesses. This is the second qualification, and it follows a

well-established principle of the Scriptures. Every divine fact that the Lord wishes to establish to the Church is validated on the basis of two or three independent witnesses. God will particularly give prophets to the apostle as witnesses.

3. *Ministers Are Given to Apostles* (Acts 20:4,5). God gives apostles other ministers to work with them in team ministry under their authority.

4. *Fully Functioning Churches* (1 Cor. 9:2). There are many persons who pioneer a church apparently successfully and with God's grace. This does not necessarily make them apostles. However, repeated success in church planting, coupled with the other characteristics above, certainly gives evidence of an apostolic call.

5. *Serious Resistance from Evil Prince Angels* (2 Cor. 12:7). Apostolic ministry can be identified by the amount of opposition it receives. This characteristic is easily overlooked and misunderstood by the Church. The Church seems to believe that ministries that are unopposed and accepted must be blessed, and that ministries that are opposed by others must have something wrong with them. Quite the contrary is true. Those ministries that lead the way in power and renewal will also find great opposition from the enemy.[1]

These five scriptural characteristics of apostolic ministry provide the Church a means of measuring claims of apostleship. Simply claiming that God has placed us in the office of apostle is not proof that this is so. Although apostles may differ in their style of ministry, they will demonstrate these five characteristics. Many who fail the test will disagree with some or all of these characteristics, but the Word of God is our final measuring line. These characteristics of the early apostles are found in the Word. We cannot settle for anything less if we are to believe in restoration.

The Apostolate

For it is written in the Book of Psalms: "Let his dwelling place be desolate, and let no one live in it"; and, "Let another take his office" (Acts 1:20).

The *apostolate* is the office or duties of an apostle. Too often we look at an individual but fail to recognize the office that individual occupies. It is important to understand that the apostolate is an office. Paul referred to his ministry as an office (see Rom. 11:13, KJV). How can people fully discharge the duties of an office if they don't understand the office and its duties? Revelation of the apostolate is necessary in order to walk fully in the authority and power of this office. I am convinced that many apostles have never operated fully in their calling because they do not fully understand the office.

As I have already stated, much of the Church has taught that the ministry of the apostle is no longer for today. The belief has been common that there were no more apostles after the death of the Twelve (plus Paul). But what many have failed to see and understand is that although the early apostles died, the office of apostleship did not cease. *The ministry of apostleship is not just a man; it is an office.*

The disciples came together to fill the vacancy left by Judas Iscariot. They were acting on the prophetic word of David in the Psalms that another should take his office. Notice that the prophetic word as quoted in Acts 1:20 identifies this ministry as an office. The import of the prophetic word was that another should fill the vacant office.

It is the will of God that someone stand in and execute the office of apostleship from generation to generation. Men die, but offices remain. This is true in the secular world as well as in the Church, as in the example of the office of President of the United States. If the president dies, the office does not die with him;

someone else takes his place. The same is true concerning the office of apostleship. Although the early apostles died, the office of apostleship remains until this day.

An office is a position of authority, duty or trust given to a person. The person in the office must faithfully administer the duties of the office. The apostle is an officer of the Church. As an officer, the apostle has duties and functions to execute.

It has always been the will of God for this office to be executed from generation to generation. It was never His will for it to be vacant. This is true concerning all the offices of the fivefold ministry (see Eph. 4:11). Most churches would not think of going too long without a pastor. They will usually try to fill that office as quickly as possible. A vacancy in the pastorate can mean trouble for a church. Someone needs to execute the duties of the pastorate.

We have thought differently, however, when it comes to the apostolate. Because many have taught that there was no more need for apostles after the death of the Twelve, this office has been vacant during much of the past 2,000 years. There are certain things that will not happen when there is a vacancy, because there is no one to stand in the office and execute its duties and functions.

We are now seeing a generation of apostles being released by the Lord to stand in this office and to execute its duties and functions. Certain individuals once again are accepting this ministry and beginning to walk in it strongly. Periodically there have been apostles throughout Church history, but now we are seeing a restoration of this ministry. This means that we will see a greater number of apostles ministering on the earth.

On every continent we are seeing believers accept this call and stand in this office. Again, this does not mean that everyone who claims apostleship is a true apostle. There are, however, many genuine apostles ministering today, and the number is increasing as our understanding of this vital office increases.

This influential office carries a tremendous amount of power and authority. God has deposited this power and authority in this office because the duties of the office require it. The power and authority vested in the apostle are in direct proportion to the responsibilities of the office. Once we understand the responsibilities of the office, we will understand why there is so much authority given to apostles.

Let's look again at the word *strateuomai*. It means to execute the duties and functions of the apostolate. Those duties and functions can be arduous. Apostolic ministry is hard work. It takes a tremendous amount of power, authority, wisdom and grace to execute the apostolate.

> But by the grace of God I am what I am, and His grace toward me was not in vain; but I labored more abundantly than they all, yet not I, but the grace of God which was with me (1 Cor. 15:10).

Paul stated that he labored more abundantly than all the other apostles. He did it by grace. In other words, he did not labor in his own strength but by God's power. The word "labored" is *kopiao*, meaning to feel fatigue, to work hard. It is from the root word *kopos*, meaning to toil, to experience pains, trouble and weariness.

The duties and responsibilities of the apostolate require great grace for abundant labor. There is a grace resident within this office for this kind of ministry. Paul described his ministry in detail:

> Are they ministers of Christ?—I speak as a fool—I am more: in labors more abundant, in stripes above measure, in prisons more frequently, in deaths often.
>
> From the Jews five times I received forty stripes minus one. Three times I was beaten with rods; once I was stoned; three times I was shipwrecked; a night and a day I have been

in the deep; in journeys often, in perils of waters, in perils of robbers, in perils of my own countrymen, in perils of the Gentiles, in perils in the city, in perils in the wilderness, in perils in the sea, in perils among false brethren; in weariness and toil, in sleeplessness often, in hunger and thirst, in fastings often, in cold and nakedness—besides the other things, what comes upon me daily: my deep concern for all the churches.

Who is weak, and I am not weak? Who is made to stumble, and I do not burn with indignation? (2 Cor. 11:23-29).

These are the things Paul went through to discharge the duties of the apostolate. Satan did everything to oppose him and keep him from executing the duties of his office. Satan hates and fears this office, because he knows its inherent power and authority. He has tried to blind the Church from a revelation of this office. He has tried, through tradition and unbelief, to blind those called into this office. He knows that once the apostolate is executed, it will mean great destruction to his plans and purposes.

Restored for a Purpose

The apostolic anointing is a laboring anointing. When Jesus sent out the Twelve, He called them workers (see Matt. 10:10). "Worker" is translated from the same word as "laborers" in Matthew 9:38. It is the Greek word *ergates*, meaning a toiler. Jesus admonished the Church to pray that He would *send forth* laborers into the harvest. Remember, *send forth* is an apostolic term. It takes this kind of laborer to bring in the harvest. Jesus connects apostolic ministry to reaping the harvest.

So I will restore to you the years that the swarming locust has eaten, the crawling locust, the consuming locust, and the chewing locust, My great army which I sent among you (Joel 2:25).

Joel prophesied about restoration of the harvest. I believe this is also a prophetic word about the restoration of apostolic ministry, because Jesus connected the harvest to the apostolic. We will see a harvest of souls in this day that will surpass the number of souls that came into the Church during its entire first 2,000 years. Much of the harvest has been eaten away because of the lack of apostolic ministry. Therefore, restoration of this ministry is necessary to reap the harvest and fulfill Joel's prophecy. The Lord is restoring this ministry, and with it the ability to labor under difficult circumstances if necessary to bring in the harvest.

Nothing can deter or stop the apostolic; it labors by grace in spite of difficult and often impossible circumstances. It presses through obstacles and brings in the harvest. It overcomes the tiredness and weariness that would stop most people. This anointing releases a supernatural ability to labor in any situation.

THE LORD PUTS HONOR UPON THE PART OF THE BODY THAT LACKS. HE IS PRESENTLY HONORING THE OFFICE OF THE APOSTLE IN THIS HOUR.

The apostle Peter preached about the times of restoration or restitution, spoken by the prophets since the world began (see Acts 3:21). He stated that heaven will receive our Lord until the times of restoration of all things is complete. There are seasons in which the Lord magnifies certain offices and restores them to the Church. Although to some degree all of the anointings and offices have been in operation since the Early Church, I am referring to the office being restored in its fullness.

There have always been those who have ministered as apostles throughout the history of the Church. The Lord, however, is restoring this office in such a way that many will be raised up to

minister as apostles in the last days. The Lord puts honor upon
the part of the Body that lacks (see 1 Cor. 12:24). The Lord is
presently honoring the office of the apostle by placing His glory
upon it for this hour.

Duties Executed by Apostles

Apostles need to know the duties and functions of the apostolate
in order to faithfully discharge them. The following duties are to
be executed by apostles:

A. *To gather.* The apostolic anointing is a gathering anointing.
   Apostles gather people for the purpose of teaching,
   training and mobilizing them to fulfill the purposes and
   plans of God. They have the charisma to attract people
   for the purposes of the kingdom. "He who is not with
   Me is against Me, and he who does not *gather* with Me
   scatters abroad" (Matt. 12:30, italics added).

B. *To impart.* Apostles have an ability to impart spiritual
   graces to the saints. This impartation enables the saints
   to fulfill their callings and destinies (see Rom. 1:11).

C. *To mobilize.* Apostles have the ability to stir up and
   mobilize the army of God. People need to be gathered
   and mobilized to fulfill the Great Commission.

D. *To order.* Apostles bring order and government to the
   Church. The apostolic anointing is a governing anointing.
   Government is necessary to facilitate the flow of God's
   power and anointing (see Titus 1:5).

E. *To judge.* Apostles bring judgment and correction to the
   Church. They issue sentences and verdicts against false
   teaching and incorrect behavior (see 1 Cor. 5:3).

F. *To reform.* Apostles are reformers. They bring the necessary
   change to the house of God. Apostles are raised up during
   times of reformation (see Heb. 9:10).

G. *To build.* Apostles are wise master builders. The apostolic anointing is a building anointing. Apostles help build strong churches. They have been likened to general contractors; they are responsible for overseeing the construction of the house of God (see 1 Cor. 3:10).

H. *To bring revelation.* Apostolic ministry is a ministry of revelation. Apostles bring insight to the Body of Christ concerning the plans and purposes of God (see Eph. 3).

I. *To father.* Apostles are spiritual fathers. As fathers they birth, protect, teach and mentor. They restore the principle of fatherhood to the Church (see Mal. 4; 1 Cor. 4:15).

J. *To lay foundation.* The apostolic anointing is a foundational anointing. Apostles lay foundation in the lives of God's people, preparing them for coming moves of God. Without apostolic ministry, people lack the proper foundation to grow properly (see Eph. 2:20).

K. *To initiate.* Apostles initiate new moves of God. The apostolic anointing is an activating anointing. Apostles are catalysts. This gift helps release the other gifts in the Church.

L. *To bridge.* Apostles are raised up during seasons of transition. They provide bridges necessary for the Church to transition from the old to the new.

M. *To establish.* Apostles help establish truth, revelation, churches and new moves of the Spirit. To establish means to bring into being on a firm or permanent basis.

N. *To pioneer.* Apostles are pioneers. They keep the Church moving into new territories, both naturally and spiritually.

O. *To legislate.* As officers of the Church, apostles legislate. They issue orders and Kingdom decrees for the Church (see Acts 15).

P. *To execute.* Apostles have a unique ability to execute the plans and purposes of God. To execute means to carry out, perform or do. This anointing is absolutely necessary to fulfill the Great Commission.

Q. *To defend.* Apostles are defenders of the faith. They defend the truth. They defend the Church from outside attacks and infiltration by the enemy (see Phil. 1:17).

R. *To oversee.* The apostolate is also called a "bishoprick" (see Acts 1:20, *KJV*). To be a bishop means to oversee. Apostles oversee churches.

S. *To invade.* Apostles invade new territories. This is a militaristic mantle. They have the ability to penetrate hostile environments with the message of the Kingdom.

T. *To war.* Apostles are territorial warriors. They are spiritual commanders of the highest rank. "Warfare" is translated from the Greek word *strateia*, meaning "apostolic career" (see 2 Cor. 10:4).

U. *To enforce.* Apostles are spiritual enforcers. They enforce Kingdom conduct, holiness and biblical standards of righteousness. To enforce means to put or keep in force, to compel obedience (see Titus 1:13).

V. *To convert.* Apostles convert people to the laws and culture of the Kingdom. They turn people from darkness to light and from the power of Satan to God (see Acts 3:19; 26:18).

W. *To train.* Apostles train and educate ministers. They develop leadership.

X. *To ordain.* Apostles ordain and set in place qualified leadership (see Titus 1:5). This includes selection and confirmation. Apostolic ordination releases fruitfulness (see John 15:16).

Y. *To confront.* Apostles confront false teaching, witchcraft, immorality, anything that will keep the Church from fulfilling its purpose. The apostolic anointing is a confrontational anointing (see Gal. 2:11).

Z. *To finish.* Apostles are focused on finishing. They have an anointing to execute, complete and fulfill the prophetic plans of God (see John 4:34).

When an apostle faithfully executes his duties, the people who have been birthed into the Kingdom and discipled by his ministry will be faithful "epistles" to all men, reflecting the apostolic dimension in such a way that they will be effective in the ministries to which God has called them.

Note

1. Roger Sapp, *The Last Apostles on Earth* (Companion Press: Shippensburg, Pennsylvania, 1995), pp. 28-37. Printed by permission.

THE APOSTOLIC CHURCH

Some of the greatest churches the world has ever known are now on the earth. Apostolic churches and apostolic networks are developing around the world as God is positioning His Church to fulfill the Great Commission.

Dr. C. Peter Wagner calls this movement a "new apostolic reformation." It is a movement that ultimately will affect everyone within the Church. The challenge to each of us is, will we fight against and reject the movement, or will we support it and flow with it? I believe that the more we understand about the apostolic dimension, the more we will want to become a part of this great end-times move of God.

Apostolic Dimension

An apostolic church is a church that has a strong apostolic dimension. A dimension is defined as the measurement in length, width and thickness. It is the proportion, extent, range, scope or weight of a thing. The apostolic dimension, therefore, is the *measure* of the apostolic anointing that is flowing through an individual believer or corporate assembly.

To be able to identify the apostolic dimension, we need to know the characteristics of the apostolic ministry. What are the distinguishing marks of true apostolic ministry? Many of these characteristics are found in the book of Acts; the apostolic anointing is the dominant anointing throughout that entire book. We identified these distinguishing marks in the last chapter, referring to them as the "apostolic seal."

If the apostolic dimension is lacking in a church, that church will lack a necessary ingredient for success. This dimension, however, is available and can be received through impartation. The ministry gift of the apostle has been given to the Church to release an apostolic dimension to all believers. When we receive the ministry of the apostle, we will receive the apostolic dimension. This does not make everyone an apostle, but it can release believers to be apostolic.

When a church becomes apostolic, it will see breakthroughs that were not possible before; there will be an ability to do things that previously could not be done. This is because of apostolic grace that is released and received through apostolic ministry. Grace gives us an ability to accomplish what we have been called and sent to do.

For example, some local churches are strong in evangelism, but weak in the prophetic. Other churches may be strong in the prophetic, but weak in evangelism. Still others may be strong in teaching, but weak in the prophetic. Churches will usually reflect the strength of its pastors, because the church receives its dimensions from its leaders.

If the pastor is a strong teacher, the church will have a strong teaching dimension. If the pastor is an evangelist, the church will have a strong evangelistic dimension. This is why believers need to be exposed to different ministry gifts; no one gift can perfect the Church.

Law of Impartation

The apostolic anointing is transferable, meaning it can be transmitted from one person to another. This is the law of impartation. When God anoints someone, there is a measure of grace placed within that individual's life. The individual then becomes a container, or reservoir, of the anointing. The Lord desires to release His anointing into the earth. Wherever and whenever the anointing flows, it brings blessings, miracles, healing and deliverance. Yokes are destroyed and burdens are lifted because of the anointing (see Isa. 10:27). The Lord has chosen to use men and women as channels to release His anointing into the earth.

The word "Christ" is derived from the Greek word *Christos*, which means anointed. *Christos* comes from the root verb *Chrio*, which means to smear or rub with oil. Jesus is the Christ—the Anointed One. He operated in the Spirit (anointing) without measure (see John 3:34). While He ministered here on earth, the anointing flowed through Him to bless the multitudes. Miracles and healings were common in His earthly ministry because of the anointing.

Through the law of impartation, Christ transferred a measure of His anointing to the disciples and sent them forth as apostles (see Luke 9:1,2). They went forth and had similar results as Jesus, because they ministered in a measure of His anointing. The Lord releases His anointing into the earth through those He calls and sends.

Apostles, prophets, evangelists, pastors and teachers are all called and sent by the Lord. They each have a dimension of Christ to impart to the Church.

Therefore He says: "When He ascended on high, He led captivity captive, and gave gifts to men" (Eph. 4:8).

In other words, when the Lord ascended He divided His mantle into five parts. He gave the apostolic mantle to some (not all). He gave His prophetic mantle to some (not all). He gave His evangelistic mantle to some (not all). He gave His pastoral mantle to some (not all). He gave His teaching mantle to some (not all).

Each mantle carries a certain amount of grace. Jesus had the

Spirit (anointing) without measure, but the ministry gifts are given according to the measure of the gift of Christ (see Eph. 4:7). The apostle receives an apostolic measure. The prophet receives a prophetic measure. The evangelist receives an evangelistic measure, and so forth. A measure means a limit or degree. No one person carries all the anointing. Different people carry different measures. Jesus measured the anointings and divided them among men.

This is God's method of getting His anointing into the earth. The apostle has received an anointing to release, because he has received a measure from Christ. The apostle can impart this to the saints. The saints then receive and are able to minister in an apostolic dimension.

The apostolic anointing flows from Jesus, through the apostles, to the saints within the earth. The same is true of the other ministry gifts. Each anointing is unique and serves a unique and important purpose, and each has certain characteristics.

If the Church receives all five dimensions by being exposed to anointed ministry gifts, it can manifest Christ to the world, because Christ's fullness is seen through all five combined gifts. Each ministry is important; we need all five dimensions. In other words, every believer should be multidimensional.

In this book, we are emphasizing the apostolic dimension. This does not mean that the others are not important or necessary. Often when the Lord is restoring a truth, there will be an emphasis on that truth (seemingly at the expense of other truths). The other dimensions are also necessary, however.

Accessing Apostolic Grace

Just as it is right for me to think this of you all, because I have you in my heart, inasmuch as both in my chains and in the defense and confirmation of the gospel, you all are partakers with me of grace (Phil. 1:7).

Because the apostolic dimension is so necessary for the local church to function properly, each local church must develop a strategy for accessing apostolic grace. There are two ways a local church can access apostolic grace. The first and primary way is to have an apostle as the senior elder (pastor) of the local church. Apostles can pastor because there is a shepherding dimension to the apostolic anointing. When the senior elder is an apostle, there will be a consistent flow of the apostolic anointing that will cause a strong apostolic dimension to be present in the local church. This is released through the preaching, teaching, prophesying and overall ministry of the apostle.

However, all pastors are not apostles. It is not necessary to be an apostle to pastor a local church. Although all pastors are not apostles, all pastors need the apostolic dimension to operate effectively in their ministries and local churches. Therefore, the second way for a local church to access apostolic grace is to be in relationship with an apostle. Through this relationship, the apostolic anointing can flow into the local church, releasing an apostolic dimension.

This does not mean an apostolic dimension will come into a local church just because some of those in the church know an apostle. There must be a strategy, a course of action that will result in accessing the grace that rests upon the apostolic office. This can include fellowship, conferences and other means to draw from the anointing upon the apostles with whom pastors are in covenant.

Dr. Noel Woodroffe of Elijah Ministries in Trinidad refers to these relationships as "Cornelius Connections." This is based upon the account in Acts 10 of Cornelius's prayers and alms coming up as a memorial before the Lord. The Lord sent an angel to Cornelius to give him instructions to contact the apostle Peter, who in turn would give him the word of salvation. The two things that opened the way for Cornelius to connect with Peter were *prayer* and *giving*.

Cornelius accessed the grace upon Peter's life through his praying and giving. Therefore, prayer and giving is a good strategy to access apostolic grace. As local churches pray for these divine connections, the Lord will supernaturally bring these relationships into manifestation. Don't go out and grab the first person who calls himself an apostle; pray for Cornelius Connections. Once a Cornelius Connection has been established, releasing finances through giving is one way to access the grace necessary to receive the apostolic dimension.

Remember the apostles' Mission: Impossible? There was no way a group of frightened and discouraged disciples—hiding in a closed room for fear of the Jews—could, without grace, fulfill the commission given to them by our Lord. Not only did they need grace, but they needed an *abundance* of grace.

And with great power the apostles gave witness to the resurrection of the Lord Jesus. And great grace was upon them all (Acts 4:33).

Grace is *the ability of God to do what ordinarily could not be done.* From the Upper Room came 120 people who would turn the world upside down. How did this small group of unknowns gain such momentum and accomplish the impossible? The answer, of course, is through grace. They were recipients of "great grace." The word "great" here is the Greek word *megas,* from which we derive our commonly used prefix "mega-," meaning very large in size or proportion. The apostles had *mega-grace.*

The apostolic anointing releases large amounts of grace to the Church. There is such a release until no gift is lacking (or falls short) in the Church (see 1 Cor. 1:4-7). Churches under this anointing will also be enriched in all utterance and all knowledge.

God's mega-grace gives the Church all the gifts and abilities it needs to fulfill the Great Commission. Without this grace, the Church will not be able to finish the work. Lack of grace means

THE CHURCH CANNOT SETTLE FOR BEING AVERAGE; OUR COMMISSION IS NOT AN AVERAGE COMMISSION.

certain failure; for this reason, the principle anointing of the Church *must* be apostolic. An apostolic company of believers will be gifted and graced to do mighty exploits. This will cause them to excel in ministry and break the chains of mediocrity.

The Church cannot settle for being average; our commission is not an average commission. Apostles and apostolic people are graced with a multitude of abilities. To have ability means that one has the necessary power, skill or resources. It means to be well fitted, equipped, competent, endowed and empowered. The Church must become staffed with competent and qualified people graced for the task.

The frustration that many churches now experience will then be broken. Mega-grace will release singers, musicians, finances, helps, property, ministries—everything necessary to get the job done.

Jerusalem—The First Church

And they continued steadfastly in the apostles' doctrine and fellowship, in the breaking of bread, and in prayers.

Then fear came upon every soul, and many wonders and signs were done through the apostles. Now all who believed were together, and had all things in common, and sold their possessions and goods, and divided them among all, as anyone had need.

So continuing daily with one accord in the temple, and breaking bread from house to house, they ate their food with gladness and simplicity of heart, praising God and having favor with all the people. And the Lord added to the church daily those who were being saved (Acts 2:42-47).

As we've already seen, the word "first" in 1 Corinthians 12:28 is the Greek word *proton*, meaning first in time, place, order or importance. The church of Jerusalem was first in time, place, order and importance. All the churches in the book of Acts were apostolic, because they were founded by or had the presence of the apostles. But the Jerusalem church had the presence of the Twelve (including Matthais, who was chosen to replace Judas Iscariot). This church would have a strong apostolic dimension because of the apostles' ministries.

The following points list some of the characteristics of the church at Jerusalem:

1. *Apostolic Doctrine.* The believers continued steadfastly in the apostles' doctrine. Apostolic teaching is foundational and needs to be in the life of every believer. Apostolic churches are known for sound doctrine based on the Word of God. Apostolic people will be people of sound doctrine.
2. *Fellowship.* This is the Greek word *koinonia*, meaning partnership, participation and communion. The apostolic dimension causes strong participation from believers when that dimension is present as believers gather together and fellowship with one another.
3. *Breaking of bread.* These were communion services. The Lord's supper was a vital part of this church.
4. *Prayers.* Prayer meetings were also a vital part of this church. The apostolic anointing releases a strong dimension of prayer into the local church.

5. *Fear.* This is the reverential fear of the Lord. *The Living Bible* says, "Terror gripped the entire church and all others who heard what had happened" (Acts 5:11). Great fear is another distinguishing mark of apostolic ministry.

6. *Signs and Wonders.* This is the miracle dimension of apostolic ministry. Signs and wonders were a part of this apostolic church.

7. *Unity.* The believers were together and had all things in common. Oneness of purpose and mind was characteristic of the church of Jerusalem.

8. *Giving.* There was a giving spirit in the church at Jerusalem. This was the result of great grace being upon them all (see Acts 4:33-35). The needs of every believer were met as a result of the apostolic dimension.

9. *Continuing Daily.* They continued daily with one accord in the Temple. They worshiped together regularly at the Temple, and they met in small groups for communion.

10. *Gladness.* Great joy, including thankfulness, was characteristic of this church. The spirit of gladness was strong in Jerusalem. Apostolic churches will have a strong Kingdom aspect of joy in the Holy Spirit (see Rom. 14:17).

11. *Praise.* Strong praise is released through the apostolic anointing. Apostolic churches will be centers of praise and celebration. Praise in an apostolic church will be instrumental in pulling down strongholds. Through praise, kings are bound with chains and nobles with fetters of iron (see Ps. 149:8).

12. *Favor.* The whole city was favorable toward them. "Favor" is the Greek word *charis*, meaning the divine influence upon the heart. God gives apostolic churches favor in their cities, regions or nations.

The result of the apostolic dimension was incredible church growth. The Lord added daily to the Church. Addition, multiplication and multitudes are common terms used in the book of Acts to refer to the growth of the apostolic church (see Acts 5:14; 6:7; 11:21).

The apostolic dimension causes and fuels church growth. Multitudes are attracted to churches that receive and walk in the apostolic anointing. I refer to this as the "apostolic draw."

Great Power and Grace

And with *great power* the apostles gave witness to the resurrection of the Lord Jesus. And *great grace* was upon them all (Acts 4:33, italics added).

The apostolic church will be a church of great power. Power is a distinguishing mark of true apostolic ministry. The Lord never sends people without giving them power. Power is necessary to accomplish the task for which one is sent. When the Lord sent the Twelve, He gave them power (*dunamis*) and authority (*exousia*).

The Greek word *dunamis* means miraculous power, a worker of miracles, power or strength. Acts 4:33 mentions "great power." As we have seen, the word "great" is *megas*, meaning big. Apostolic ministry is characterized by *mega-power*, as well as *mega-grace*. This is a dimension of power that is beyond the norm. The result will be an unusually large number of healings and miracles. The powers of darkness will be blasted by great power from on high. I call this the "apostolic blast."

Apostolic (sent) people will witness with great power. The Church cannot properly witness to the world that "Jesus is alive!" without the apostolic dimension.

The apostolic church is also a church of "great grace." The Greek word *charis* means divine influence upon the heart. Grace moves people because it moves their hearts. The result of great grace in the context of Acts 4:33,34 was giving. The saints sold their possessions and laid the money at the apostles' feet. This was done without compulsion and was simply the result of great grace.

Paul identifies giving as a grace (see 2 Cor. 8:2-7). It is the nature of grace to give. The apostolic anointing will release a divine influence upon the heart that will manifest itself in giving. An apostolic church will have great grace for giving, with abundant finances released for the work of the ministry.

Abundance is the result of grace. The apostolic dimension will cause needs to be met because it releases abundance.

Signs and Wonders

And through the hands of the apostles many signs and wonders were done among the people (Acts 5:12).

An apostolic church will be a church of signs and wonders. Signs and wonders are mentioned throughout the book of Acts. The apostolic anointing is the dominant anointing in the book of Acts, where seven characteristics of signs and wonders are found:

1. Signs and wonders reveal God's approval upon ministry (Acts 2:22).
2. Signs and wonders are a mark of an apostolic church (Acts 2:43).
3. Signs and wonders release God's people to minister in boldness (Acts 4:30,31).
4. Signs and wonders touch the common man (Acts 5:12).
5. Signs and wonders follow a sent one (Ps. 105:26,27; Acts 7:36).
6. Signs and wonders attract people (Acts 8:13).
7. Signs and wonders give testimony to God's Word (Acts 14:3).

Signs and wonders are the mark, or seal, of an apostle (see 2 Cor. 12:12). The Lord bears witness to the apostle's ministry through signs and wonders (see Heb. 2:4). A valid ministry must have the Lord's approval and witness, and signs and wonders validate a true apostolic ministry. This is a part of the apostolic seal upon believers who receive and walk in an apostolic dimension. Signs and wonders are a part of the apostolic witness.

From Darkness to Light

> When He had said these things, He spat on the ground and made clay with the saliva; and He anointed the eyes of the blind man with the clay. And He said to him, "Go, wash in the pool of Siloam" (which is translated, Sent). So he went and washed, and came back seeing (John 9:6,7).

Siloam means *sent*. The pool of Siloam is a type, or prophetic symbol, of apostolic ministry. The blind man returned from the pool seeing. Spiritual blindness is common because everyone is born blind. Sent ones bring light to those in darkness. Apostolic ministry penetrates darkness, causing spiritual eyesight to return. Every believer needs the ministry of a sent one to be able to see clearly.

Sent ones have an anointing that brings revelation to the Church. Notice that Jesus anointed the blind man's eyes with clay made in part with saliva. This represents the anointing touching the eyes of the blind. There are certain truths that the Church will never see without this anointing.

Wherever the apostolic dimension is strong, there will be an apostolic pool (Siloam) from which people will come away seeing. The Lord is providing spiritual basins where His people can come and wash. These are reservoirs of the anointing containing a concentration of the apostolic spirit that can open the eyes of the multitudes. Apostolic churches are places where this anointing will be found in concentration.

If people want to see, they must obey the command of the Lord to go and wash in the pool. If the blind man had not obeyed, he would not have received his sight. He obeyed the Sent One and received his miracle. The apostolic anointing causes recovery of sight to the blind (see Luke 4:18).

"I will deliver you from the Jewish people, as well as from the Gentiles, to whom I now send you, to open their eyes, in order to turn them from darkness to light, and from the power of Satan to God, that they may receive forgiveness of sins and an inheritance among those who are sanctified by faith in Me" (Acts 26:17,18).

These are the words of the Lord Jesus to Paul. The apostle was sent to open the eyes of the Gentiles and to turn them from darkness to light. This was Paul's commission. He knew his purpose and was focused on what he was sent to do.

Multitudes of people live in spiritual darkness, groping about under the dominion of Satan who has blinded their minds (see 2 Cor. 4:3,4). They are in need of deliverance from spirits of blindness, darkness and ignorance. The Lord, in His mercy, sends apostles with an anointing that will destroy the yokes of bondage (see Isa. 10:27).

Satan savagely opposes the apostolic ministry, persecuting it because of the massive damage it inflicts on his kingdom. The apostolic anointing penetrates the darkness and removes the veil that is spread over the nations (see Isa. 25:7). An apostolic church is a threat to the spirits of darkness that control a city, region or nation.

The apostolic dimension begets unveiled believers—believers who can see and will walk in the revelation this ministry brings. One of the distinguishing marks of true apostolic ministry is *revelation*.

By revelation He made known to me the mystery (Eph. 3:3).

By revelation the Lord makes known the mysteries of His kingdom. Paul understood the secrets of the Kingdom because he received revelation. Resident within the apostolic anointing is the spirit of revelation; those who receive and walk in this dimension will receive a strong measure of revelation.

You can measure the apostolic dimension by the extent of revelation in which an individual believer or local church walks. Where the apostolic dimension is lacking, so is understanding of the mysteries of the kingdom of God.

"Revelation" in Ephesians 3:3 is the Greek word *apokalupsis*, meaning a disclosure or manifestation. It comes from the root word *apokalupto*, meaning to take off the cover, to disclose or to reveal. Things hidden from the foundation of the world are revealed during apostolic times.

> Which in other ages was not made known to the sons of men, as it has now been revealed by the Spirit to His holy apostles and prophets (Eph. 3:5).

Apostles and prophets receive revelation by the Spirit. Through the law of impartation they impart this revelation to the saints so they, too, may understand the mysteries of the Kingdom. There is a grace upon these ministries to cause believers to see the mysteries being revealed (see Eph. 3:9).

Paul referred to himself and other apostles of his day as "stewards of the mysteries of God" (1 Cor. 4:1). *The Living Bible* says, "So Apollos and I should be looked upon as Christ's servants who distribute God's blessings by explaining God's secrets."

As we wash in the apostolic pool, we will come away seeing. The saints will have revelation and insight into the mysteries of the Kingdom. They will possess spiritual understanding and wisdom in the things of God. They will not walk in ignorance and darkness, but in knowledge and light.

The Signs of an Apostle

Truly the signs of an apostle were wrought among you in all patience, in signs, and wonders, and mighty deeds (2 Cor. 12:12, *KJV*).

An apostolic (sent) people are a people of *patience*. The Greek word for "patience" in the above passage is *hupomone*, meaning cheerful, endurance and constancy. It means to continue in spite of persecution, tribulation or resistance. The apostolic dimension gives the saints the ability to overcome obstacles and demonic opposition through patience.

BOLDNESS IS NECESSARY TO OVERCOME THE THREATS AND INTIMIDATION OF DEMONS—AND THE RELIGIOUS SYSTEMS THAT OFTEN ATTACK A MOVE OF GOD.

Patience also means perseverance. The ability to persevere and overcome the pressures of the enemy is a characteristic of an apostolic church. Paul, in defending his apostleship, mentioned those things he endured (see 2 Cor. 11:24-29).

The enemy is not able to overcome an apostolic church because of the force of patience. No matter how much he attacks that church, he cannot defeat it when the saints receive and walk in the apostolic dimension.

Now when they saw the boldness of Peter and John, and perceived that they were uneducated and untrained men, they marveled (Acts 4:13).

Apostolic (sent) people are a people of *boldness*. The words "bold," "boldly" and "boldness" are mentioned throughout the book of Acts (see, for example, Acts 4:13; 9:27; 14:3; 18:26; and 19:8). Boldness is necessary to overcome the threats and intimidation of demons, as well as the religious systems that often attack a move of God. The word "boldness" is translated from the Greek word *parrhesia*, meaning all outspokenness, frankness, bluntness, assurance and confidence.

There is a spirit in the world that attempts to prevent the Church from being bold and aggressive in witnessing. Satan attacks believers with fear, and tries to keep them from being aggressive and going forth in fulfilling the Great Commission. The apostolic dimension gives the saints the boldness they need to overcome this spirit.

> But Peter and the other apostles answered and said: "We ought to obey God rather than men" (Acts 5:29).

Apostolic (sent) people are a people of *obedience*. The sent one's desire is to obey the Sender. Grace and apostleship are given for obedience to the faith among all nations (see Rom. 1:15). The apostolic anointing caused many priests to become obedient to the faith (see Acts 6:7).

The apostolic dimension will cause the saints to become obedient to the Word of God in all areas. It is also a deterrent to disobedience and rebellion. Apostolic people are not afraid to obey God in spite of opposition from men or religious systems. The apostles continued to preach the truth despite being told not to by the religious leaders of their day (see Acts 4:18-21).

Apostolic Covering

> This is the will of the Father who sent Me, that of all He has given Me I should lose nothing, but should raise it up at the last day (John 6:39).

The apostolic anointing provides a covering (protection) for those who submit to it. It is not the will of God that believers be lost to backsliding, the world, the flesh or the devil.

The apostolic dimension provides a bulwark against the schemes and wiles of the enemy. The apostolic anointing is a "keeping anointing" (see John 17:12). It provides the ability to maintain and keep what has been committed to us. When this anointing is lacking, much of the fruit and ground gained over time is lost. When the early apostles died, much of the fruit and ground gained in the book of Acts was lost; the Church entered a period of darkness that lasted more than a thousand years.

Apostolic Draw

No one can come to Me unless the Father who sent Me *draws* him; and I will raise him up at the last day (John 6:44, italics added).

Jesus depended on the Sender, the Father, to draw men to Himself, the Sent One. Apostolic (sent) people depend upon the Lord to draw people. I also call this the "apostolic draw" or "supernatural draw." People are attracted to apostolic ministry by the Spirit of God. Multitudes are drawn, not by the work of a person, but by the work of the Lord. There is a divine pull that works through an apostolic people.

Apostolic churches have the ability to draw many people because the apostolic anointing is a gathering anointing. This accounts for the often quick growth of these churches. People are drawn by the churches' message and witness. This drawing power is resident within the apostolic anointing. "A multitude gathered from the surrounding cities to Jerusalem, bringing sick people and those who were tormented by unclean spirits, and they were all healed" (Acts 5:16).

Apostolic Examples

And Stephen, full of faith and power, did great wonders and signs among the people (Acts 6:8).

And the multitudes with one accord heeded the things spoken by Philip, hearing and seeing the miracles which he did (Acts 8:6).

Stephen and Philip are mentioned among the six who were chosen by the church in Jerusalem to be over the daily ministration (see Acts 6:5).They were not called apostles, yet they were obviously ministering in an apostolic dimension. Philip is later referred to as an evangelist (see Acts 21:8). They operated and ministered in the realm of miracles. Stephen is noted further for the wisdom with which he spoke (see Acts 6:10).

Both Stephen and Philip came out of an apostolic community. They were present at the church in Jerusalem; both had gifts of working of miracles. But beyond their gifts they also had received an apostolic dimension. This is an example of how believers are affected by the apostolic anointing.

Philip was able to leave Jerusalem, minister to Samaria and see tremendous breakthroughs in the city. He was able to penetrate the veil of darkness there because he walked and ministered with the apostolic dimension. Apostolic churches have an ability to raise up, train and release strong ministers. Apostolic churches produce apostolic people. God is raising up an apostolic company of believers and sending them forth into the earth.

Now when the apostles who were at Jerusalem heard that Samaria had received the word of God, they sent Peter and John to them (Acts 8:14).

The Jerusalem church was also a sending church. They sent

Peter and John to Samaria when they heard of the Samaritan people receiving the Word of God. Apostolic churches will send ministers where there are needs. Although the Samaritans had believed and been baptized, they needed the apostles to come and lay hands upon them to be filled with the Holy Spirit. Sending churches have an ability to help believers receive and walk in a greater dimension of the Holy Spirit.

Antioch: A Sending Church

> And the hand of the Lord was with them, and a great number believed and turned to the Lord. Then news of these things came to the ears of the church in Jerusalem, and they sent out Barnabas to go as far as Antioch (Acts 11:21,22).

The Jerusalem church sent Barnabas to Antioch when they heard of the numbers of people that were receiving the Lord. The church at Antioch was founded by a group of believers who were scattered during the persecution in Jerusalem. These believers, like Stephen and Philip, came out of an apostolic community. The church at Antioch had an apostolic dimension, a dimension strengthened by the arrival of Barnabas from Jerusalem.

Antioch became a teaching center after Barnabas brought Paul to assemble the believers there for an entire year (see Acts 11:26). The church at Antioch was a church filled with grace (see Acts 11:23). This church also became a place where prophets and teachers ministered (see Acts 13:1). As they ministered to the Lord and fasted, the Holy Spirit instructed them to separate Barnabas and Saul for the ministry of apostleship.

> Then, having fasted and prayed, and laid hands on them, they sent them away (Acts 13:3).

The church of Antioch became a *sending church*. Barnabas and

Paul were sent forth as apostles (sent ones) from Antioch. From Antioch was launched one of the greatest apostolic ministries of all time. As a result of the sending forth of Barnabas and Saul—later, Silas and Paul—hundreds of churches were planted all over the known world. Antioch became a spiritual hub for apostles, prophets and teachers. Present there was an atmosphere conducive for the Spirit of God to separate and release ministries into the earth.

Apostolic churches will have an apostolic spirit. Remember, the Holy Spirit is an apostolic Spirit. He is sent by the Father, and He sends ministries. Antioch is an example of a sending church operating in a strong apostolic dimension.

> So, being sent out by the Holy Spirit, they went down to Seleucia, and from there they sailed to Cyprus (Acts 13:4).

Barnabas and Saul were sent forth by the church at Antioch and by the Holy Spirit. Notice that the Holy Spirit works in conjunction with the Church in sending ministries. Sent ones are successful because they have the backing of the Church and the Lord. The apostolic spirit works through the apostolic church to release powerful ministries into the earth.

The Macedonian Churches: Apostolic Distribution

> Moreover, brethren, we make known to you the grace of God bestowed on the churches of Macedonia: that in a great trial of affliction the abundance of their joy and their deep poverty abounded in the riches of their liberality (2 Cor. 8:1,2).

Paul commended the churches of Macedonia for their liberal giving despite their poverty. Paul attributed this to grace. Remember, great grace is a manifestation of the apostolic anointing. Grace is the divine influence upon the heart that is often manifested through giving.

Paul called this giving a "liberal sharing" or distribution (see 2 Cor. 9:13). The apostles in the Jerusalem church distributed to or shared with the saints in need (see Acts 4:32-37). I refer to this as "apostolic distribution." There was no lack in this church because of this distribution.

Apostolic churches serve as distribution centers. The apostolic anointing has within it a grace for finances. We see this manifested when the saints laid money at the apostles' feet (see Acts 4:37). Apostolic churches are able to release large amounts of finances into the places where there is the greatest need.

Paul was receiving an offering for the saints in Jerusalem from the churches of Philippi, Thessalonica and Corinth. These Gentile churches were encouraged to give to their Jewish brothers and sisters who were lacking because of a famine in Judea. This offering was important because it would cause the Jewish church to see that the Gentiles professed subjection to the gospel of Christ.

Missions should be a high priority in apostolic churches because this is a part of the apostolic mandate (see Acts 13:47). We are called to help existing churches in other nations, and to help to plant new ones. Apostolic churches have a great responsibility to properly use and distribute the wealth that this anointing draws. To whom much is given, much is required (see Luke 12:48).

As it is written, "He has dispersed abroad, He has given to the poor; His righteousness endures forever" (2 Cor. 9:9).

CHAPTER NINE

APOSTOLIC
AUTHORITY

And when He had called His twelve disciples to Him,
He gave them power over unclean spirits,
to cast them out, and to heal all kinds of sickness
and all kinds of disease.

MATTHEW 10:1,2

The first thing Jesus gave the Twelve when He sent them out was *power.* Yet power is the one thing many Christians lack. The reason for that is because they don't understand the connection between authority and power. If you truly want to walk in power, then you must first learn to walk *in* and *under* authority.

"Power" in this passage is not *dunamis,* but the Greek word *exousia,* meaning ability, privilege, force, capacity, competency, freedom, mastery, delegated influence, authority, jurisdiction, strength. Author Paula A. Price, in her book *God's Apostle Revived,* writes:

Apostles exude authority. Active or dormant, their authority is difficult to disregard. It is the first obvious distinguishing feature. Whatever the situation the apostle inevitably stands out. He unavoidably finds himself in charge or it is thrust upon him. He competently makes decisions and often casts the deciding vote. Apostles lead when they do not try to; are looked to and relied upon when others seek a strong hand. They command attention and provoke obedience because of God's blatant authority upon them. Extended involvement with an apostle puts you face to face with authority.[1]

Faithful Ambassadors

I concur with Price that authority is one of the distinct marks of an apostle and an apostolic church. This authority is recognized in the spirit realm by angels and demons alike. It is released through preaching, teaching, prophesying and the overall ministry of the apostle. And it is desperately needed by the Church to fulfill the Great Commission.

Without apostolic authority, the Church will be unable to complete its mission. The kingdom of God is established and maintained through authority. It is expanded through authority that dispels darkness and sets the captives free.

When the Twelve were sent out, our Lord Jesus entrusted them with power. They were given authority over unclean spirits and sickness. They were official representatives of Christ, given authority by Him, as His ambassadors, to preach the gospel, heal the sick and cast out devils.

An ambassador is an official delegate or representative, speaking for and representing the nation or organization from which they have been sent. They are given official authority to act in this capacity. This will give you some idea of the tremendous authority given to the Twelve as representatives of Christ. They had an awesome responsibility to represent the Lord correctly as His ambassadors.

An ambassador is further defined as an official envoy, a diplomatic agent or delegate of the highest rank accredited to a foreign government. A delegate is simply one person acting for another. The Twelve were sent forth as official delegates of Christ, with delegated power and authority. They formed an apostolic delegation. They had specific instructions in what to do and what not to do. They had to follow these instructions because they were not representing themselves, but Christ.

A wicked messenger falls into trouble, but *a faithful ambassador brings health* (Prov. 13:17, italics added).

Faithful apostles bring healing and deliverance with their message. They will speak with power and authority because of whom they represent, but they must be faithful to the message committed to them. They are sent by the Lord, not man. This may cause them to fall out of favor with some, but they must be faithful to the One who sent them.

Zechariah's Vision

Then I raised my eyes and looked, and there were four horns. And I said to the angel who talked with me, "What are these?" So he answered me, "These are the horns that have scattered Judah, Israel, and Jerusalem."

Then the Lord showed me four craftsmen [carpenters]. And I said, "What are these coming to do?" So he said, "These are the horns that scattered Judah, so that no one could lift up his head; but the craftsmen are coming to terrify them, to cast out the horns of the nations that lifted up their horn against the land of Judah to scatter it" (Zech. 1:18-21).

In this vision, Zechariah saw four horns, which represented the four powers that had scattered Israel. The horn is a symbol of power, strength and might. There are powers in every region whose purpose is to scatter people and prevent them from gathering.

I have talked to countless pastors who are frustrated because they cannot seem to gather together a strong group of believers.

Many see their churches grow to a certain size and then split or diminish because of something that occurs. This could be strife, division, rebellion or any number of things that come against the church to scatter the flock. Until these horns are dealt with, the people will remain scattered and not be able to *lift up their heads*.

This represents oppression and bondage. There are multitudes of people in despair politically, economically and spiritually. They cannot lift themselves out of their situations because these horns are in place. The powers of darkness are determined to keep the multitudes in this condition.

The prophet then sees four craftsmen, or carpenters. These carpenters come to fray the horns. These four carpenters represent the apostolic. A carpenter is a builder; the apostolic anointing is a building anointing. However, it is impossible to successfully build without first dealing with the horns. If the horns are not destroyed, they will continue to thwart the building process.

The carpenters have the authority and power to destroy the horns and cast them out. The term "cast out" is a deliverance term. Multitudes are delivered as a result of the coming of the carpenters. The *Amplified* translation says, "But these smiths or workmen have come to terrorize them and cause them to be panic-stricken, to cast out the horns or powers of the nations who lifted up their horn against the land of Judah to scatter it."

These carpenters have an anointing with power and authority to terrify and cast out these powers. The Lord is releasing the apostolic anointing in full measure upon the Church. He is raising up apostolic churches that will terrify the horns that have ruled regions for so long. Apostolic prayer, preaching, teaching, praise and worship come with tremendous amounts of power and authority to break the power of ruling spirits that have tried to hinder the growth and expansion of the Kingdom.

Then I raised my eyes and looked, and behold, a man with a measuring line in his hand. So I said, "Where are you going?" And he said to me, "To measure Jerusalem, to see what is its width and what is its length."

And there was the angel who talked with me, going out; and another angel was coming out to meet him, who said to him, "Run, speak to this young man, saying: 'Jerusalem shall be inhabited as towns without walls, because of the multitude of men and livestock in it'" (Zech. 2:1-4).

The prophet then sees a man measuring Jerusalem. Why is the man measuring Jerusalem? Because a harvest is coming after the horns have been destroyed. Multitudes will gather in Jerusalem because the scatterers have been cast out by the carpenters.

The Lord wants to know the capacity of our local churches. What is the length and breadth of your ministry? What are the spiritual dimensions of your church? Can our local churches really handle the multitudes that will come? Do we have the capacity to nurture, teach and train them? Are we poised for church growth?

The apostolic anointing has the power and authority to destroy and cast out the powers of darkness that hinder church growth. Multiplication will take place once this anointing is received and released. Local churches will grow and experience the blessing of the Lord. Entire regions will be impacted by the gospel. The saints will gather to worship and praise the King!

The Reality of Witchcraft

The book of Acts—the Acts of the Apostles—provides the model for the New Testament Church. Again, the dominant anointing in the book of Acts is the apostolic anointing. Although the other gifts are mentioned, the apostolic office is the one that the Holy Spirit chose to highlight. There is a reason for this. The Holy Spirit is first and foremost an apostolic Spirit. He is a *sent* Spirit. The Church, as the book of Acts illustrates, is to be, first and foremost, apostolic.

The *acts of the apostles* continued after the death of the early apostles. As God raises up other apostles to replace them, the acts continue. The Church, therefore, will experience the same results when it embraces the same spirit and anointing.

Among the dark spirits we must contend with today is a spirit of witchcraft. Witchcraft is one of the major forces confronting the Early Church throughout the book of Acts (see Acts 8; 13; 16; 19). Why did the Holy Spirit choose to record these incidents? Are they simply historical incidents, or do they relate to the Church's opposition today?

Witchcraft is a common spirit, encountered in every people group in one form or another. It cannot be overlooked if we are to see breakthroughs in new territories and expand the kingdom of God. Witchcraft is a major spirit that will challenge and attempt to stop the progress of the Church. The apostolic anointing, however, has the authority and power to deal with witchcraft. It exposes, challenges and overcomes this spirit, enabling the Church to accomplish its mission in spite of spiritual opposition.

> But Peter said to him, "Your money perish with you, because you thought that the gift of God could be purchased with money! You have neither part nor portion in this matter, for your heart is not right in the sight of God. Repent therefore of this your wickedness, and pray God if perhaps the thought of your heart may be forgiven you" (Acts 8:20-22).

This is the first recorded instance of the apostolic anointing dealing with witchcraft. Simon the sorcerer believed the preaching of Philip, was baptized and followed his ministry. Upon the arrival of Peter and John from Jerusalem, the believers were filled with the Holy Spirit through the laying on of hands. Simon desired to purchase the ability to impart the Holy Spirit, but he was rebuked by Peter.

THE APOSTOLIC ANOINTING RELEASES THE DISCERNMENT THE CHURCH NEEDS TO RESIST INFILTRATION OF THE ENEMY.

The apostle discerned Simon's heart and rebuked him for his unrighteous request. The apostolic anointing releases the discernment the Church needs to resist infiltration of the enemy. This is important because it provides safety and protection for the Church against the wiles of the devil, especially witchcraft.

Witchcraft must be discerned and judged. If not, it will bring harm to the Church, especially new believers. Apostolic authority is needed to confront individuals who operate in this spirit. This keeps the Church pure and free from spiritual contamination.

There are many who do not see or understand the subtle nature of witchcraft. It can creep into a church undetected when the apostolic anointing is not present.

O foolish Galatians! Who has *bewitched* you that you should not obey the truth? (Gal. 3:1, italics added).

Signs of Witchcraft

One of the signs of witchcraft operating and infiltrating a church is the inability of the people to obey the truth. Disobedience and rebellion are always present wherever there is witchcraft. People can start off obeying the truth, then later abandon it. Paul said the Galatians had been bewitched (see Gal. 3:1). In other words, there was a spiritual power that was causing them to turn from the truth. They had come under the spell of false teachers and were turning from the truth that Paul had preached to them.

False doctrine and false teachers carry a spirit of witchcraft. There is no other explanation as to why people come under the control of false teaching that is contrary to the Scriptures. The apostolic anointing keeps us free from the fascination of false teaching. It exposes the doctrines of devils and keeps the Church walking in the truth.

Some believe that witchcraft is no threat to a Spirit-filled church, but this is exactly the atmosphere that the enemy targets. Simon was fascinated by the move of God in Samaria. Wherever there is a move of the Spirit, the enemy will attempt to come in. The Galatians were born-again, Spirit-filled believers. This church had been birthed through Paul's ministry. Later, Paul wrote to them in distress, telling them they had been bewitched, or placed under a spell.

People don't know when they have been bewitched. It is usually a slow and subtle process, not something that is obvious to those who are being bewitched. Most churches that have come under this kind of influence do not recognize when it has occurred.

Are you so foolish? Having begun in the Spirit, are you now being made perfect by the flesh? (Gal. 3:3).

This is another way to detect the operation of witchcraft. There are many believers and churches who start with a mighty move of God's Spirit, only to end up years later completely in the flesh. Witchcraft attempts to move people away from trusting and following the Holy Spirit into depending upon the flesh. In the context of the Galatian church, it was legalism. They were attempting to be perfect by being circumcised and keeping the law of Moses. Paul said they were being bewitched.

I have seen churches and even entire denominations move away from the anointing and start depending on the flesh to do the work of God. Many have lost the Holy Spirit's power and are only a shell of what they once were. How does this happen? How do people who begin in the Spirit try to perfect their lives and ministries in the flesh? I believe that witchcraft often is the reason. It can slip in undetected and work slowly over a period of time.

Dealing with Witchcraft

This is one of the reasons we need an apostolic anointing present within the Church. This anointing deals with witchcraft. It helps keep the Church walking in and depending upon the Holy Spirit. The apostolic anointing prevents the enemy from stopping the flow of the Spirit.

> But Elymas the sorcerer (for so his name is translated) withstood them, seeking to turn the proconsul away from the faith. Then Saul, who also is called Paul, filled with the Holy Spirit, looked intently at him and said, "O full of all deceit and all fraud, you son of the devil, you enemy of all righteousness, will you not cease perverting the straight ways of the Lord? And now, indeed, the hand of the Lord is upon you, and you shall be blind, not seeing the sun for a time." And immediately a dark mist fell on him and he went around seeking someone to lead him by the hand (Acts 13:8-11).

I like the way Paul dealt with witchcraft. He did not play around with it. He judged it with the power of God, calling down blindness upon Elymas the sorcerer. This type of authority and judgment is returning to the Church with the restoration of apostolic ministry.

With the restoration of the apostolic ministry, we will see the same manifestations return to the Church that we read about in the book of Acts: people falling down dead, sorcerers smitten with blindness, leaders being eaten up by worms. This is not a pleasant picture, but the Lord will allow no man or woman to hinder the preaching of the gospel in these last days.

> Now it happened, as we went to prayer, that a certain slave girl possessed with a spirit of divination met us, who brought her masters much profit by fortune-telling. This girl followed Paul and us, and cried out, saying, "These men are servants of the Most High God, who proclaim to us the way of salvation."
>
> And this she did for many days. But Paul, greatly annoyed, turned and said to the spirit, "I command you in the name of Jesus Christ to come out of her." And he came out that very hour (Acts 16:16-18).

This is the only apostolic deliverance that is given in detail in the book of Acts. Why did the Holy Spirit choose to detail this deliverance for us to read? I believe this deliverance gives us some important truths concerning the apostolic anointing and what the Church will encounter in fulfilling the Great Commission.

This damsel was possessed with a spirit of divination, another form of witchcraft. This is the third example in the book of Acts where the apostles dealt with witchcraft.

The Greek word for witchcraft is *python*. A python is a large constrictor. Constrictors kill their prey by slowly squeezing the breath out of them. There are believers, churches and entire regions that are bound by python spirits, lifeless as a result of witchcraft, sorcery and divination. Breath represents spirit. The Greek word for both breath and spirit is *pneuma*. Python spirits attempt to squeeze the life out of the Church by stopping the flow of the Holy Spirit.

There is no free flow of the Holy Spirit where python spirits are allowed to operate, therefore there are no manifestations of the Holy Spirit. When this happens there is no life in the Church, because the Holy Spirit is the Giver of spiritual life and must be free to move among and through His people.

The apostolic anointing breaks the power and grip of python spirits. The result is a free flow of the Holy Spirit and spiritual life. The saints are then released to operate in the gifts of the Spirit, thus opening the way for strong prayer, praise, worship, prophecy, miracles, healings and deliverance. Apostles are anointed to break the powers of darkness and keep the Church free from the snares of the devil.

> And many who had believed came confessing and telling their deeds. Also, many of those who had practiced magic brought their books together and burned them in the sight of all. And they counted up the value of them, and it totaled fifty thousand pieces of silver (Acts 19:18,19).

This is the fourth example from the book of Acts of the apostolic anointing breaking the power of witchcraft. The *New English Bible* translation says, "They openly confessed that they had been using magical spells." This public burning of books was a total renunciation of Satan and his kingdom.

Dr. C. Peter Wagner has said, "I wonder what new doors to evangelism might be opened in sophisticated, tolerant, politically-correct America if Christians started expressing their faith by encouraging those who possessed artifacts of magic or unclean books to burn them publicly." With the proliferation of psychics and new age teachings in America and around the world, the Church must embrace the apostolic and begin to operate in this dimension if we are to see the kinds of breakthrough experiences recorded in the book of Acts.

Witchcraft must be confronted and dealt with. The Church

cannot ignore witchcraft and hope it will go away. We must have an anointing to discern and confront this spirit whose assignment is to stop and hinder the Church. An apostolic Church will possess the power and authority to overcome this spirit and to advance in spite of its opposition.

Note

1. Paula A. Price, *God's Apostle Revived* (Everlasting Life Publications: Plainfield, New Jersey, 1994).

A BLUEPRINT FOR APOSTOLIC LIVING

Therefore, indeed, I send you prophets, wise men,
and scribes: some of them you will kill and crucify, and
some of them you will scourge in your synagogues
and persecute from city to city.

M A T T H E W   2 3 : 3 4

God has left us a blueprint for apostolic living, and we find it in the Scriptures. We as the end-times Church would be wise to study and heed that blueprint. Here we will look at some Old Testament figures who represent the apostolic dimension and show us personal applications to each of our lives as believers. The writer of Romans tells us, "Whatever things were written before [in the Old Testament] were written for our learning" (Rom. 15:4).

Jesus mentions prophets, apostles and scribes as being sent ones. Apostles are also referred to as wise men in Matthew 23:34. Paul referred to himself also as a wise master builder (see 1 Cor. 3:10). Luke's account mentions the "wisdom of God" speaking as the Sender of the apostles (Luke 11:49). In other words, prophets, apostles and scribes are sent by the wisdom of God. To reject these ministries is to reject the very wisdom of God.

The eighth chapter of Proverbs delineates the attributes and benefits of wisdom. These include excellent things, right things, truth, instruction, prudence, knowledge, discretion, counsel, understanding, strength, riches, honor, righteousness, blessing, life and favor. All these things are released through the ministry of a sent one.

Sent ones come in the Spirit of the Sender. If they are sent by the wisdom of God, they will come in the Spirit of wisdom. An apostolic people will walk in and manifest a spirit of wisdom—wisdom necessary to build properly.

The Church is to manifest this wisdom to the principalities and powers in heavenly places (see Eph. 3:10). In other words, the Church, through wisdom, should impact the spirit realm. Those exposed to apostolic ministry will receive and walk in a higher level of wisdom. The Church cannot be built without wisdom.

Through wisdom a house is built, and by understanding it is established (Prov. 24:3).

Apostolic and prophetic wisdom are necessary to build the Church, the house of the Lord, not just globally but on a local level, too. Every local church needs the apostolic dimension to build properly. The Church must be built according to God's ordained pattern. The blueprint must be obtained by the Spirit; it must be received by revelation.

Moses

And let them make Me a sanctuary, that I may dwell among them. According to all that I show you, that is, the pattern of the tabernacle and the pattern of all its furnishings, just so you shall make it (Exod. 25:8,9).

Moses was instructed by the Lord to build the sanctuary according to the pattern he received. It was not left up to human wisdom to build the sanctuary. The Church cannot be built properly with human wisdom and skill; the blueprint must come from heaven. God's plan for His Church is quite different from the plan of man. Churches that are built without apostolic wisdom and revelation will have constructional cracks and faults, which the enemy will exploit.

Moses is a *type*, or prophetic symbol, of apostolic ministry. He received the pattern from the Lord to build a sanctuary to God's specifications. Just as the dimensions and details of the sanctuary were given to Moses by revelation, so apostles bring patterns to the Church. They are wise master builders, spiritual architects. They receive wisdom and grace to know and implement God's blueprint for His Church. Apostolic wisdom is necessary if we are to build properly.

Then the Lord spoke to Moses, saying: "See, I have called by name Bezalel the son of Uri, the son of Hur, of the tribe of Judah. And I have filled him with the Spirit of God, in wisdom, in understanding, in knowledge, and in all manner of workmanship, to design artistic works, to work in gold, in silver, in bronze, in cutting jewels for setting, in carving wood, and to work in all manner of workmanship" (Exod. 31:1-5).

And Bezalel and Aholiab, and every gifted artisan in whom the Lord has put wisdom and understanding, to know how to do all manner of work for the service of the sanctuary, shall do according to all that the Lord has commanded (Exod. 36:1).

Wisdom is the key to building the sanctuary properly. Bezalel and Aholiab were men of skill, men of ability who were filled with wisdom. They brought beauty and excellence to the sanctuary. The house of the Lord should be a place of excellence. Everything about it should reflect the beauty and excellence of the Lord.

The apostolic dimension releases the wisdom necessary to build according to God's pattern. The result will be a Church of beauty and excellence, reflecting the glory and wisdom of the Lord.

Nehemiah

Nehemiah is also a type of apostolic ministry. His name means "Comforter"; he is a type of the Holy Spirit. Remember, the Holy Spirit is an apostolic Spirit because He was sent by the Father (see John 14:26). Nehemiah was also a sent one.

And I said to the king, "If it pleases the king, and if your servant has found favor in your sight, I ask that you send me to Judah, to the city of my fathers' tombs, that I may rebuild it." . . . So it pleased the king to send me; and I set him a time (Neh. 2:5,6).

Nehemiah was sent to build. The apostolic spirit is a building spirit. Whenever you find the apostolic dimension, you will find building or rebuilding. In spite of opposition, Nehemiah was able to rebuild the walls of Jerusalem because he was sent; he had authority from the king to build.

Nehemiah also shows us that where there is building, there will be warfare. He commanded his builders to hold weapons in one hand and building equipment in the other. Even today, there is no building without warfare. Satan will always oppose the building of the Church. Apostolic churches are warfare churches that are able to fight through opposition and build.

And they shall rebuild the old ruins, they shall raise up the former desolations, and they shall repair the ruined cities, the desolations of many generations (Isa. 61:4).

This is the result of the ministry of a sent one. Isaiah prophesied about our Lord, "The Spirit of the Lord God is upon Me, because the Lord has anointed Me to preach good tidings to the poor; He has sent Me to heal the brokenhearted" (Isa. 61:1). The anointing upon sent ones causes rebuilding to occur.

Tabernacle of David

> But now your kingdom shall not continue. The Lord has sought for Himself a man after His own heart, and the Lord has commanded him to be commander over His people, because you have not kept what the Lord commanded you (1 Sam. 13:14).

> And when He had removed him, He raised up for them David as king, to whom also He gave testimony and said, "I have found David the son of Jesse, a man after My own heart, who will do all My will" (Acts 13:22).

The Tabernacle of David is a type of the apostolic Church, and David is a type of the apostolic ministry. Today, through the restoration of the apostolic Church, God is rebuilding the Tabernacle of David.

The Tabernacle of David will have the spirit of David. (The spirit here is the essential nature of a person or a group, an attitude or principle that inspires or pervades thought, feeling or action.) David was the sweet psalmist of Israel (see 2 Sam. 23:1). David was also an anointed minstrel (see 1 Sam. 16:23). When he played, Saul was refreshed. Anointed minstrels release *refreshing*. To refresh means to give new freshness or brightness, to restore, to fill up again, to replenish, to revive.

Saul was also made well or whole. This is *healing*. The evil spirit departed from him when David played the harp. The spirit of David is a spirit of *deliverance* (see 1 Sam. 16:23).

David was *cunning* in playing. Cunning means executed with or exhibiting ingenuity. It means skill or adeptness in execution or performance. Ingenuity means inventive skill, imagination or extraordinary creative ability.

David was also a *mighty, valiant* man, courageous and bold in battle. He was a man of war, and he was *prudent*. Prudent means wise in handling practical matters; exercising good judgment or common sense. It also means to be careful about one's conduct, or circumspect. Circumspect means heedful of circumstances and potential consequences.

David was also a handsome or *comely* person, pleasing and wholesome in appearance. He was attractive (see 1 Sam. 16:18).

David reigned and executed judgment and justice over Israel (see 2 Sam. 8:15). He was a fair man, a man of justice.

David was a seeker and worshiper of God. He loved the presence of God. He feared God, yet he was a fighter. David was a champion.

Obviously David's Tabernacle would have his spirit; he was its founder and builder. We should see the same spirit of David in the apostolic Church today.

> After this I will return and will rebuild the tabernacle of David, which has fallen down; I will rebuild its ruins, and I will set it up (Acts 15:16).

Amos prophesied that the Lord would rebuild the Tabernacle of David (see Amos 9:11). David raised up this Tabernacle and gave Israel a pattern of worship. Remember, apostles bring patterns to the Church. David is a type of apostolic ministry in that he left for Israel a pattern of worship.

The Tabernacle of David was simply a tent erected by him in which the ark of God was placed. Surrounding this tent were musicians and singers who praised the Lord continually.

> So he left Asaph and his brothers there before the ark of the covenant of the Lord to minister before the ark regularly, as every day's work required (1 Chron. 16:37).

This was prophetic worship established by David.

Moreover David and the captains of the army separated for the service some of the sons of Asaph, of Heman, and of Jeduthun, who should *prophesy* with harps, stringed instruments, and cymbals . . . who *prophesied* according to the order of the king (1 Chron. 25:1,2, italics added).

Prophetic worship includes new songs, spontaneous songs and prophetic songs. It releases the psalmists and minstrels to flow prophetically in the house of the Lord. The Tabernacle of David provides an atmosphere for the glory of the manifest presence of God, and the Lord's presence brings healings, miracles and deliverances.

The Tabernacle of David represents true worship. This is worship that is done in spirit and in truth (see John 4:24). Our worship should have a prophetic dimension because the Holy Spirit is also a prophetic Spirit.

As Israel continued to backslide and worship idols, the Tabernacle began to fall down. Israel forsook the true worship of God and took up idolatry. The Tabernacle of David eventually ended in ruins, though Amos prophesied of the day it would be rebuilt.

Solomon's Temple

David left a pattern for future generations, a pattern of worship that would fall into ruin and be restored by kings such as Hezekiah and Josiah. David also left to his son Solomon the pattern to build the Temple. He received this pattern by the Spirit:

Then David gave his son Solomon the plans for the vestibule, its houses, its treasuries, its upper chambers, its inner chambers, and the place of the mercy seat; and the plans [pattern] for all that he had by the Spirit, of the courts of the house of the Lord, of all the chambers all around, of the treasuries of the house of God, and of the treasuries for the dedicated things;

"All this," said David, "the Lord made me understand in writing, by His hand upon me, all the works of these plans [pattern]" (1 Chron. 28:11,12,19).

The house of God was built according to *pattern*. When local churches are not built according to heavenly pattern, they will not contain the glory that is released when built correctly. When Solomon finished building, the Lord confirmed the building with His manifest presence (see 2 Chron. 5:14). Apostolic churches will have the manifest presence of God because they are built with apostolic wisdom, according to a heavenly pattern.

Hezekiah

Moreover King Hezekiah and the leaders commanded the Levites to sing praise to the Lord with the words of David and of Asaph the seer. So they sang praises with gladness, and they bowed their heads and worshiped (2 Chron. 29:30).

Hezekiah was a type of apostolic ministry in that he *restored* davidic worship to Israel. The Tabernacle of David was central to Israel's worship, and the apostolic dimension causes a rebuilding of this Tabernacle.

Restoration is resident within the apostolic dimension. Things that the Church has lost over a period of time are restored. As we discussed earlier, these are referred to as "times of restoration" (see Acts 3:21). Apostolic times are times of restoration and restitution. The Church needs the apostolic dimension to be able to build the old places, raise up the former desolations and repair cities that lay waste.

The result of the Tabernacle of David being restored is that the Gentiles might seek after the Lord (see Acts 15:16,17). When true worship is restored to the Church, the nations will be affected, and sinners will be drawn to the Church.

Amos also prophesied that the saints would possess the remnant of Edom and all the heathen. This is a prophetic word concerning possessing the nations with the kingdom of God. It speaks of the advance of the Kingdom. This is why the Tabernacle of David must be and is being rebuilt through the apostolic anointing.

Hezekiah restored stature to the house of God. Whenever the house of God loses its stature in the earth, the Lord will raise up apostolic ministries to restore it.

Joseph

> And God sent me before you to preserve a posterity for you in the earth, and to save your lives by a great deliverance (Gen. 45:7).

These are the words of Joseph. He realized he had been sent by the Lord into Egypt, ahead of his family, to preserve for them a posterity in the earth.

Sent ones preserve a posterity, meaning all future generations collectively. So apostolic ministry affects future generations. Apostolic ministry stops destruction, causing spiritual life to be maintained from one generation to the next. The move of God would cease without sent ones.

Joseph described the salvation of his family as "a great deliverance." The apostolic dimension has resident within it a deliverance anointing. The ability to deliver those appointed to death is characteristic of a sent one's ministry. When the Church loses the apostolic dimension, it loses its posterity.

Joseph delivered Israel in time of famine. Without Joseph, Israel would have died. Instead, they were fed and preserved. The sent one feeds and preserves.

He sent a man before them—Joseph—
Who was sold as a slave.
They hurt his feet with fetters,
He was laid in irons.
Until the time that his word came to pass,
The word of the LORD tested him.
The king sent and released him,
The ruler of the people let him go free.
He made him lord of his house,
And *ruler* of all his possessions,
To *bind* his princes at his pleasure,
And *teach* his elders wisdom
(Ps. 105:17-22, italics added).

Joseph was made a ruler in Egypt. The apostolic dimension has resident within it the ability to rule.

Joseph was given authority over Egypt's wealth. He had the wisdom necessary to rule over Pharaoh's possessions. The apostolic dimension gives the Church the wisdom to rule over the earth.

Joseph was also given authority to bind Pharaoh's princes. Binding and loosing is another function of the apostolic anointing. To bind means to arrest, stop, hinder or tie up. Binding is necessary to stop the works of darkness. Apostolic authority is needed to arrest, stop, hinder and tie up the powers of darkness that attempt to hinder the advance of the kingdom of God. Demons must recognize the authority of sent ones. When the Church receives and walks in the apostolic dimension, there will be an increase of authority in binding.

Joseph was also given the responsibility to teach Pharaoh's senators wisdom. Teaching is another manifestation of the apostolic dimension. Sent ones release wisdom into the Church for ruling and administrating. This is a governmental wisdom needed in the local church.

Pharaoh's senators needed wisdom to fulfill their governmental functions. Today, the apostolic dimension is needed to teach wisdom to the leadership of the local church. Apostolic churches are places where our future leaders are trained and taught wisdom.

APOSTOLIC CHURCHES ARE PLACES WHERE FUTURE LEADERS ARE TRAINED AND TAUGHT WISDOM.

Governmental giftings—the fivefold ministries in Ephesians 4:11—are trained in an apostolic church for future ministry.

Joseph went into Egypt ahead of his family. He was sent to prepare the way for them to come after him. There was a grace upon his life to endure the trials and sufferings he had to go through before he reached his place of authority.

Uzziah

Most Christians are familiar with certain aspects of the ministry of the twelve apostles under the compassionate guidance of the Son of God. In fact, the Word of God identifies apostles as forerunners—those who go first—in the kingdom of God (see 1 Cor. 12:28). Someone who is first will set an example for others to follow. An apostle is a *progenitor*.

A progenitor is defined as a person or thing that originated something or serves as a model. It is from the Greek word *genetor*, meaning a model for others to follow. As such, apostolic ministry is a pioneering, foundation-laying ministry. An example of this type of ministry can be found in the life of Uzziah, an Old Testament king.

Let us look at the rise and demise of Uzziah. What he did and accomplished during his reign was extraordinary and amazing, to say the least. The key to his success was seeking the Lord.

He sought God in the days of Zechariah, who had understanding in the visions of God; and as long as he sought the Lord, God made him prosper (2 Chron. 26:5).

Uzziah is an example of someone who prospered by seeking the Lord. His life is an example for us to follow. Apostles and apostolic people must give themselves to prayer (see Acts 6:1-7). Those who seek God will meet with tremendous results in ministry. The life of Uzziah is a type of apostolic ministry that prospers by seeking God.

Warfare

Now he went out and made war against the Philistines, and broke down the wall of Gath, the wall of Jabneh, and the wall of Ashdod; and he built cities around Ashdod and among the Philistines (2 Chron. 26:6).

Uzziah went forth and *warred* against the Philistines. Apostolic ministry is a ministry of warfare. Principalities and powers over cities and nations must be attacked and defeated by men of authority. Apostles have the ability to go forth and war against the enemy.

Uzziah was a God-fearing king of Judah who exercised his *authority* against the enemy. Seeking God releases the authority and anointing for warfare.

Breaking Down Walls

Walls represent barriers that keep the truth of the gospel out. Walls separate and divide. We need to break down walls of tradition, religion, prejudice and racism.

When walls are built around a city, they are meant to keep out invading forces. Uzziah broke down the walls of Gath, Jabneh and Ashdod, the cities of the Philistines. He was able to enter and subdue these cities by breaking down their walls.

Satan and his principalities build walls around cities in an attempt to keep the people in bondage and to keep the truth out.

Like Jericho, many cities are shut up, and the people are walled in. Apostolic ministry has the ability to tear down these walls and invade the strongholds of the enemy. The result is the salvation of multitudes and the planting of strong New Testament churches.

Not only did Uzziah tear down, but he built. Building cities in the midst of Philistia is a type of building churches in the midst of the enemy.

Supernatural Assistance

God helped him against the Philistines, against the Arabians who lived in Gur Baal, and against the Meunites (2 Chron. 26:7).

The Lord helped Uzziah against his enemies. Supernatural help and assistance will follow true apostolic ministry. The Lord releases his angelic army to assist His anointed against the enemy, thus giving the apostle the ability to overcome even the greatest opposition. Nothing is impossible for those who have supernatural assistance.

No matter how strong or organized the enemy may be, he can be overcome and defeated by sent ones with supernatural assistance. This was a key to Uzziah's success against his enemies. Seeking God releases the Lord's supernatural aid and assistance against the enemy.

Attracting Wealth

Also the Ammonites brought *tribute* to Uzziah. His fame spread as far as the entrance of Egypt, for he became exceedingly strong (2 Chron. 26:8, italics added).

Tribute is a stated sum or other valuable consideration paid by one sovereign or state to another in acknowledgment of subjugation or as a price of peace. Wealth is released when the enemy is defeated and subjugated. There are spoils (goods) that are captured once the enemy is defeated.

Jesus talked about spoiling the strongman's house after he is bound (see Matt. 12:29). Apostolic ministry will plunder the goods of the enemy and release wealth into the Kingdom. As a result of Uzziah's ever-increasing wealth, his name was spread abroad, and he strengthened himself exceedingly.

In the midst of warfare, apostolic ministry will grow stronger. In the midst of opposition, it will grow stronger. The Church in the book of Acts grew stronger and stronger despite persecution and opposition.

Strengthening the Gates

And Uzziah built towers in Jerusalem at the Corner Gate, at the Valley Gate, and at the corner buttress of the wall; then he fortified them (2 Chron. 26:9).

Apostles are gatekeepers, guarding the points of entry into a city. Whoever controls the gates will control entry into and exit from the city. Uzziah built towers on the gates in order to position soldiers and watchmen to guard and protect the gates of Jerusalem.

Apostles not only attack the enemy, but they strengthen the Church's gates in defense against attack. Our gates must be fortified against attack from Satan.

Building and Digging

Also he built towers in the desert. He dug many wells, for he had much livestock, both in the lowlands and in the plains; he also had farmers and vinedressers in the mountains and in Carmel, for he loved the soil (2 Chron. 26:10).

Apostles have the ability to build in desert places. Desert places represent dry places in the Spirit. There are many cities and nations that are spiritually dry; there is no flow of the Spirit. There is a lack of refreshing teaching and preaching.

Uzziah dug many wells. This is a strength of apostolic ministry: the ability to dig wells in dry places. A well is not haphazardly dug. It takes skill to know where and how to dig a well. Churches established through apostolic ministry will become wells in dry places. They will be points of refreshing in the midst of dry places of religion and tradition.

Note that Uzziah had large herds; he also had the ability to sustain these herds. Apostolic ministry will provide sustenance for large numbers of people. Large flocks will not be uncommon in these days as the Lord raises up apostolic ministry.

Husbandry

Uzziah "loved the soil." The *King James Version* uses the word "husbandry." Four important components of husbandry are plowing, sowing, pruning and reaping.

Apostles know how to plow the fallow ground through their preaching and teaching. They plow through tradition and anything that would keep the soil of men's hearts from being broken up.

They then sow the Word into the hearts of men. Once the ground is broken up, the Word can be sown into the heart; once the Word is sown, it will bring forth fruit. After the plowing and sowing comes the pruning.

Pruning is necessary to insure a healthy plant. To prune means to rid or clean of anything superfluous or undesirable. Pruning is rebuking and correcting. It is an unpleasant but necessary part of husbandry.

Apostles rebuke and correct. Their preaching eliminates those undesirable traits in the people of God. After pruning, the vine brings forth fruit abundantly.

This is harvest time. Reaping comes after plowing, sowing and pruning. This is apostolic ministry as typified by Uzziah— *plowing, sowing, pruning* and *reaping.*

Army of God

> Moreover Uzziah had an army of *fighting men* who went
> out to war by companies (2 Chron. 26:11, italics added).

Apostolic ministry attracts *fighting men*. Remember, it is a ministry of
warfare. The Lord is raising up an army, and apostles have the ability
to recruit, gather and train people for warfare. Not only do they train
warriors but also captains (leadership) to be over God's army.

These mighty warriors will be strong and courageous with the
ability to make war and help their leaders against the enemy (see
2 Chron. 26:15). They enable the apostolic ministry to overcome
principalities and powers, to break through spiritual opposition
and to build.

> Then Uzziah prepared for them, for the entire army,
> shields, spears, helmets, body armor, bows, and slings to
> cast stones (2 Chron. 26:14).

Uzziah gathered, trained and *equipped* his army to defeat the
enemy. Apostolic ministry equips the saints to fight. Apostles
train the saints to use the weapons of warfare, including the
Word, prayer, fasting, deliverance, binding and loosing.

These weapons are not carnal but mighty through God to the
pulling down of strongholds (see 2 Cor. 10:4). Uzziah made prepa-
ration for his army. He prepared the weapons for his soldiers.
Apostles must prepare the weapons for the army of God by teaching
God's people to put to use the spiritual weapons He has provided.

Divine Strategies

> And he made devices in Jerusalem, invented by skillful
> men, to be on the towers and the corners, to shoot arrows
> and large stones (2 Chron. 26:15).

Uzziah was a pioneer in the field of warfare, pioneering new methods to fight the enemy. This is also true concerning apostolic ministry. As we have seen, apostles have a pioneer anointing. They will do things that others have not done, venturing into realms where others have not gone.

Although we have attended numerous seminars and heard much teaching on spiritual warfare, there is still more to learn. Even now there are divine strategies from heaven being released into the earth. The Lord is revealing new ways to defeat the enemy. Apostles will tap into this revelation and release it to the Church through preaching and teaching.

The Danger of Pride

But when he was strong his heart was lifted up, to his destruction (2 Chron. 26:16).

This verse reveals a major weapon the enemy will use to stop strong apostolic ministry: *pride.* Apostles are susceptible to the spirit of pride. Any ministry that accomplishes so much is in danger of becoming "lifted up." This was the downfall of Uzziah. His name became great as he became strong, but pride was his weakness and his downfall.

Apostles must walk in humility and avoid falling into the snare of pride. Uzziah became a leper and was cut off from the house of the Lord. Apostles must guard against pride and presumption. Pride goes before destruction (see Prov. 16:18). The *New English Bible* says, "[Uzziah's] fame spread far and wide, for he was so wonderfully gifted that he became very powerful."

It is difficult to be wonderfully gifted and powerful, yet not yield to pride. But the trap of pride can be escaped if apostles recognize and remember that their gift is by the grace of God.

Apostles must give God all the glory and humble themselves under His mighty hand in order to be preserved—as must we all.

For God has promised that when we humble ourselves "under the mighty hand of God," He will exalt us "in due time" (1 Pet. 5:6).

I believe this is God's time to exalt His Church; that He is raising up His apostles to accomplish just that. May we humble ourselves and walk in a renewed understanding and appropriation of the apostolic dimension, as He has called us to do.

APOSTOLIC SPIRIT: A SENDING SPIRIT

God Is a Sending God

And God said to Moses, "I AM WHO I AM." And He said, "Thus you shall say to the children of Israel, 'I AM has sent me to you'" (Exod. 3:14).

Yet He sent prophets to them, to bring them back to the Lord; and they testified against them, but they would not listen (2 Chron. 24:19).

And the Lord God of their fathers sent warnings to them by His messengers, rising up early and sending them, because He had compassion on His people and on His dwelling place (2 Chron. 36:15).

He sent a man before them—Joseph—who was sold as a slave (Ps. 105:17).

He sent Moses His servant, and Aaron whom He had chosen (Ps. 105:26).

Since the day that your fathers came out of the land of Egypt until this day, I have even sent to you all My servants the prophets, daily rising up early and sending them (Jer. 7:25).

Behold, I will send you Elijah the prophet before the coming of the great and dreadful day of the Lord (Mal. 4:5).

There was a man sent from God, whose name was John (John 1:6).

For God did not send His Son into the world to condemn the world, but that the world through Him might be saved (John 3:17).

And we have seen and testify that the Father has sent the Son as Savior of the world (1 John 4:14).

Jesus, the Greatest Apostle

To you first, God, having raised up His Servant Jesus, sent Him to bless you, in turning away every one of you from your iniquities (Acts 3:26).

Jesus Sent His Disciples

These twelve Jesus sent out and commanded them (Matt. 10:5).

Behold, I send you out as sheep in the midst of wolves (Matt. 10:16).

After these things the Lord appointed seventy others also, and sent them two by two before His face into every city and place where He Himself was about to go (Luke 10:1).

So Jesus said to them again, "Peace to you! As the Father has sent Me, I also send you" (John 20:21).

The Holy Spirit Is Sent

But the Helper, the Holy Spirit, whom the Father will send in My name, He will teach you all things, and bring to your remembrance all things that I said to you (John 14:26).

And because you are sons, God has sent forth the Spirit of His Son into your hearts, crying out, "Abba, Father!" (Gal. 4:6).

The Holy Spirit Sends

So, being sent out by the Holy Spirit, they went down to Seleucia, and from there they sailed to Cyprus (Acts 13:4).

The Church Sends

Now when the apostles who were at Jerusalem heard that Samaria had received the word of God, they sent Peter and John to them (Acts 8:14).

Then news of these things came to the ears of the church in Jerusalem, and they sent out Barnabas to go as far as Antioch (Acts 11:22).

Then it pleased the apostles and elders, with the whole church, to send chosen men of their own company to Antioch with Paul and Barnabas, namely, Judas who was also named Barsabas, and Silas, leading men among the brethren (Acts 15:22).

Paul the Apostle Sends

But I trust in the Lord Jesus to send Timothy to you shortly, that I also may be encouraged when I know your state (Phil. 2:19).

Yet I considered it necessary to send to you Epaphroditus, my brother, fellow worker, and fellow soldier, but your messenger and the one who ministered to my need (Phil. 2:25).

And [I] sent Timothy, our brother and minister of God, and our fellow laborer in the gospel of Christ, to establish you and encourage you concerning your faith (1 Thess. 3:2).

False Apostles and Prophets: Those Who Are *Not* Sent

And the Lord said to me, "The prophets prophesy lies in My name. I have not sent them, commanded them, nor spoken to them" (Jer. 14:14).

I have not sent these prophets, yet they ran. I have not spoken to them, yet they prophesied (Jer. 23:21).

For they prophesy falsely to you in My name; I have not sent them, says the Lord (Jer. 29:9).

Then some of the itinerant Jewish exorcists took it upon themselves to call the name of the Lord Jesus over those who had evil spirits, saying, "We exorcise you by the Jesus whom Paul preaches."

Also there were seven sons of Sceva, a Jewish chief priest, who did so. And the evil spirit answered and said, "Jesus I know, and Paul I know, but who are you?" (Acts 19:13-15).

Demons recognized both Jesus and Paul because they were *sent ones*. The spirit realm must recognize and contend with the power and authority of sent ones. Sent ones have the ability to impact the spirit realm. On the other hand, demons don't recognize those who are not sent.

Prayer Releases the Apostolic Anointing (Spirit)

Therefore pray the Lord of the harvest to send out laborers into His harvest (Matt. 9:38).

Then He said to them, "The harvest truly is great, but the laborers are few; therefore pray the Lord of the harvest to send out laborers into His harvest" (Luke 10:2).